Meetings and Partings

Longman Imprint Books

Meetings and Partings

Sixteen short stories compiled by
Michael Marland CBE MA
Headmaster, North Westminster Community School, London
Honorary Professor of Education, Warwick University

edited with questions by **Alison Leake**

photographs by
Catherine Shakespeare Lane

Longman

LONGMAN GROUP LIMITED
Longman House, Burnt Mill, Harlow, Essex CM20 2JE, England
and associated companies throughout the world

This edition first published 1984

ISBN 0 582 22311 3

Printed in Singapore by
Huntsmen Offset Printing (Pte) Ltd

Contents

A Certificate for Life-saving

by Sid Chaplin

"Ike's lad" thought he'd been cursed with two left hands and feet that would stumble over a matchstick. When he moved to a colliery town at the age of ten, he took an interest in swimming. He hoped to get glory as a life-saver. But it was years later that he discovered his greatest glory had actually been back in his hopeless days in the village.

A Certificate for Life-saving

When I was 10 we packed all our furniture into a colliery lorry and moved from a village in the wilderness to a bigger one that not only had a main street and a cinema with a panotrope[1] but a swimming baths built of yellow brick and supplied with water from the pit power station. The baths made a different lad of me.

In the old village I'd been cursed with two left hands and feet that would stumble over a matchstick or a bent hairpin. My brain was numb. I moved through life in a stupor wondering what would hit me next. Even my father, normally the mildest of men, went momentarily out of his mind the day I limped home after exchanging a couple of pair of partridges for a free ride in a motor car to a remote hamlet many miles away. "You've as many brains as a shallot!" he cried.

The swimming baths changed me. I floated the very first time in. It was bliss to feel the water pulsing through my fingers and let my whole body relax and go under the sky. Here was an element which was wholly friendly, and which warmed and upheld me. I could do no wrong. At the end of the first season I won the one length underwater, carried off the junior breast-stroke championship (the three lads in front were disqualified on account of using sidestroke), and also passed my lifesaving certificate with distinction. Overnight I became famous. Even the teacher rested his hand on my shoulder and praised me. "Always remember your gift," he said. "Some day, somewhere, somebody's life might depend upon you."

It was these words that finally corrupted me. I began to look for a life to save. As the volunteer lifeguard my round consisted of the claypit pond, the colliery reservoir, and the deep Mill Dam down at the river. I used to cycle furiously from one to another, wearing my costume under my clothes for readiness and praying the Lord to give me just one life to save. The Lord never obliged.

---

[1] *panotrope*: an electrical apparatus which reproduced the sound of a record through a loudspeaker

In the end I was driven to blue all my pocket money on Sunday excursions to the seaside. I used to walk miles along the sands with my shoes slung over my shoulder and with my hands ready to unfasten my belt the moment the cry went up. The nearest I got to my ambition was a girl with a bleeding foot who said she wasn't going to let me find *her* pressure point — she would rather bleed to death.

I almost gave up. Only the certificate, nicely framed by my father and now hanging in the kitchen, kept me going. During the winter months I'd often look up at it. The old itch for fame would again take possession of me. One fine day I'd pull two, perhaps even three, out of the water, then go on to swim the Channel in record time.

Came the next summer and the Lord, who must have been nodding, suddenly decided to take a hand in the matter. It happened one Saturday afternoon at the claypit pond. There was one swimmer at the far side of the pond. He started yelling and sank out of sight. A second later his head reappeared, bobbing like a turnip on the sun-dappled waters, his mouth extended in a silent scream. As I plunged in still wearing my shirt I was vaguely aware of the one other person present rapidly sprinting round the side of the pond. He had a squashed strawberry face and had been sitting down picking at his toenails. There was I struggling with a shirt that impeded every movement, and there was the toenail-picker going the quickest way — by land.

All the same I beat him. Only it didn't go in the textbook way. The victim wrapped his arms and legs around me and took me repeatedly under water. Coming up the third or fourth time he actually bit me and I slapped him back hard. He went limp. I'd just got him nicely turned over when the toenail-picker jumped from half a dozen yards away and rammed me right on the ribs. Then he shoved me with his feet. Then he calmly took the victim away from me and methodically proceeded for shore.

The crowning insult was when he waded back for me. "Come on, you're nearly there," he said as he helped me to the shore. By this time a crowd had gathered. The crowd cheered. For the first time I discovered what hate was all about.

I put the wet shirt in my saddlebag and wore my pullover next to my naked skin, then stole away. I rode ten miles with my head down and my feet hard on the pedals and tried to sweat it out, but I never did. Years later, I found myself saying to a slewed, cynical old doctor that I wished I had just one life to my credit. "Do you now?" he said with a lift of one corner of his mouth and one eyebrow. "Have you ever thought that it mightn't be altogether to your credit?"

That was a long time later. In the meantime, my botched job of life-saving took a lot of living down. My one consolation was that the toenail-picker, the thief, wasn't recommended for a medal and didn't even get a commendation. I began to shun the water. Bound to the pedals of a fixed-wheel model, I cycled miles on my own and put a spurt on whenever I was passing a pond, a lake, or a river. But I failed to sweat out that shameful memory.

It must have been a couple of summers later that three of us took some girls on an excursion to Scarborough. I was working, but this was a Bank Holiday. And we came to the open-air swimming pool and one of my mates said: "He's a champion swimmer and diver, y'know. That high board's nothing to him." I said it was a pity I hadn't brought my costume and towel. The girls pointed out that they could be hired. They wanted me to dive from the top board. It took a century to climb and when I reached the top and looked down I nearly came back. The pool was a tiny blue square and I could scarcely see the blurred white faces of my companions as they looked up and waved encouragement. Nobody will ever know the nerve it took to walk that board when all my instincts screamed to sit down and straddle my legs over it and inch myself along.

I took off in a perfect belly flapper that cut through my middle as I hit the water and surfaced slowly with a feeling that all my guts were hanging out. Gone was my intention of giving my companions a demonstration of the Australian crawl. Nobody shouted, nobody cheered, and if my arms came over in slow motion while my feet gave only an occasional flutter this was because every muscle had been pulled out of position and every bone broken if not dislocated. One of my companions knelt down and helped me over the side, smiling his relief. "I thought we were going to have to run to get somebody to pull you out, just like at the claypit pond," he said. I looked at him. The sun was blazing but the day had lost its shine.

That put me back into my old dazed condition once again. Only I was worse than when I lived in the village in the wilderness. I hurt other people as well as myself. So, in the end, I got out and took my hook,[1] taking my toll on job after job until at last I found something that suited me. The sickness vanished. But I never went near the water again.

And the years rolled on, I grew prosperous and skilful in hiding my discontent with what I'd become, inside as well as out. Then one day I got into my car and I drove to that village in the wilderness: the one where I was cursed with two left hands and feet that would stumble over a matchstick or a bent hairpin. And I walked up the street where I used to live. It was just the same as it had ever been; forlorn, grey and gritty, each house with its coalhouse and outside netty. Some still had their old zinc bathtins hanging outside. It was as if I had only left yesterday. Only I couldn't remember the number of the house we'd lived in, so I took a long shot and asked an old lady who was standing looking over the top of her yard gate.

She said of course she did, it was number 21 and what's more you're their eldest lad. "If I live to be a hundred," she said, "I shall never forget you and what you did for our Harry when you pulled him out of the river."

"You must be thinking of my brother," I said.

"No, it was you. Our Harry walked in over his head always a dare-devil, and you went in after him and managed to get hold of a hand and pull him out of the hole." She shook her head. "Fancy you forgetting a thing like that!"

"You're mistaking me for my brother," I said.

"You come in," she said. She took me into the kitchen. An old man sat in a rocking chair beside the fire. "This is Ike's lad that lived in number 21," she said. "Looks more like his Dad," he said, as he brought his face close to mine. "Well, well. The lad that saved our Harry!"

They showed me Harry's photograph. The features were unknown to me. I couldn't remember pulling him from out of the river. They gave me my tea. Everything in that house was mine for the asking. But somehow I couldn't feel a glow. The record had been sponged out so completely that I couldn't bring myself to believe that, long before I learned to swim, win races and certificates, and ache for fame, I had already saved one life. The life-saver was a different being. He'd vanised with the boob

---

[1] *took my hook*: went away

who had two left hands and feet that would stumble over a spent match or a bent hairpin. I know about the one I saved. But where is the boy I killed?

I Likes Screech, I Does

by Peter Tinniswood

Three boys in Wales with nothing to do on Bonfire Night. By following the leader they nearly kill themselves. After the horrors of this night, though, life will never be the same for any of them.

I Likes Screech, I Does

It was Bonfire Night.

We lived in Cardiff.

My dad worked on the docks.

We were bored, Spike Lewis, Soapy Rodgers and me.

Soapy's as black as the ace of spades. His dad comes from Antigua. That's in the West Indies. I read about it once.

We'd mitched[1] the day off school.

Well, when you're fifteen what else is there to do?

A rocket exploded in the sky at the back of the Mountstuart pub.

It sent out spangles of silver and gold.

"I hates Bonfire Night, I does," said Spike Lewis.

"Why?" I said.

"Because there's too many bastards enjoying theirselves. Dads with nippers letting off roman candles. Mams making welsh cakes special. It's all a load of crap, mun."[2]

He put up both his nicotine-stained thumbs and smiled.

"Everything's a load of crap. Right?" he said.

And he cackled. I never did like that cackle. It was like a rattlesnake on them crappy comboy films you sees on HTV.

"Right then," said Spike Lewis. "What'll we do now, boys?"

We were kicking a can around on the open ground behind the New Sea Lock.

"Don't know," said Soapy Rodgers. "Have a fag, is it?"

"Why not?" I said, so we lit a Sweet Afton and passed it round.

It was cold.

It was growing dark, too.

Oystercatchers piped out on the mudflats. A cormorant flew low towards Steepholm.

I likes birds, me.

When I gets the chance, I reads about them in books.

"I wouldn't half fancy a pint of Brain's Dark," said Spike Lewis. "Go in the New Sea Lock and see if Danny'll serve us

---

[1] *mitched*: truanted
[2] *mun*: man

one, is it?"

"Cor blimey, Charlie," I said. "My dad'd bloody murder me, if he caught me drinking beer."

Spike Lewis cackled again.

"Mine couldn't give a monkey's," he said.

He couldn't neither.

Well, I don't suppose you bothers with things like that when you've still got eighteen months to go in Bristol nick.

"Let's have a boat trip," said Soapy Rodgers.

"Don't be a dum dum all your life," said Spike Lewis. "The Campbell steamer has stopped running a good three months by now."

"I don't mean that," said Soapy Rodgers. "I knows where there's a rowing boat, see. We can nick it and go for a trip in the bay."

Spike Lewis looked at me.

I looked at him.

I paused.

I knew what I should say.

I didn't though.

"Why not?" I said, so we had a good spit and set off to find the boat.

It was round the back of the Pier Head we found it. Close by the new Maritime Museum. It wasn't a rowing boat in the accepted sense of the word. It was more like a bloody great whaler only the stern — that's the back of the boat, see — was sort of curved in on itself.

I thinks they call it a coble.

I read about it once in a book.

Still, it don't matter a monkey's one way or the other, if the truth be known.

It was tied to an iron ring by a bit of rope. We untied it and tried to drag it to the water's edge. It wouldn't budge.

"What'll we do now, boys?" said Soapy Rodgers. "Go back to the New Sea Lock, is it?"

"Don't be bleeding daft," said Spike Lewis. "If a job's worth nicking, it's worth nicking proper."

We heaved, and we tugged. We cursed, and we sweated, and after half an hour or so we got it into the water.

We was knackered by then, so we lit another Sweet Afton.

"The wind's getting up," said Soapy Rodgers. "Let's go to the Marl and let off a couple of rockets."

Spike Lewis cackled.

"Losing your bottle,[1] is it, Soapy?" he said.

"No," said Soapy Rodgers. "No, Spike. It's just that I nicked these two rockets off my sister, see. Be a sin to see them go to waste, right?"

"Bleeding rockets," said Spike Lewis. "What a load of crap."

He looked down at the boat, and he kicked it with the toe of his boot.

"I names this boat the SS *Daitanic*," he said. "God bless all what sails in her."

I laughed. But I felt a flutter in my guts, and my cheeks started to twitch.

It was pitch dark by now.

You could see lights twinkling on the derricks of a tanker sitting high in the dry dock. You could see the lights glowing in the back room of the Red House across the other side of the bay. They sort of shimmered on the water.

The wind was rattling things.

It began to rain.

A tug boat heaved itself out of the lock gates and blew this long mournful note on its siren.

Dead sad.

"I thinks I got a touch of diarrhoea coming on," said Soapy Rodgers.

"Come on," said Spike Lewis. "Push."

So we climbed into the boat, pushed off and the tide began to carry us out into the bay.

It went quick, too.

The water skidded along the hull of the boat. The bow rose high.

"You know what we could do with now?" said Spike Lewis.

"No," I said. "What?"

"A pair of oars."

"Cor blimey, Charlie, hasn't we got no oars?" I said.

"No," said Spike Lewis. "I just looked."

He cackled.

"Smashing, eh?" he said.

In the pitchy darkness I could see the whites of Soapy's eyes. I couldn't see his teeth.

Well, I don't suppose he was grinning if the truth be known.

---

[1] *bottle*: nerve

I wasn't.

I was shit scared.

By now we could feel the rush of water coming down from the Taff, and the boat began to rock.

"Sit still," snapped Soapy Rodgers.

"I am sitting still," I shouted.

But I wasn't. I was shivering like hell, if the truth be known.

The tide snatched us up quicker.

I saw a bonfire and fireworks being let off on the muddy beach outside the Red House pub. It was a party for the nippers. My mam and dad took me there once. I wished I was there now. I wished I was anywhere else, but on this boat.

We passed the point where the River Ely flows into the bay, and the wind began to billow and blow.

Behind us there was a bloody big bonfire on Caerphilly mountain and rockets speared into the sky. It reminded me of this hymn of the blokie what asks God for a spear of gold and arrows of desire and things like that.

I likes singing hymns, me. There's something religious about it, I thinks.

"Smashing crack, this, eh?" said Spike Lewis.

Soapy Rodgers jumped.

"What's that?" he said.

"I says it's a belting boat trip," said Spike Lewis.

Soapy Rodgers said nothing.

He just rolled his eyes.

The waves began to roll us, too.

The bow was high and the water hit under it with a smack and threw spray all over us.

Three gulls wheeled and mewed above us.

"Way, hay," screamed Spike Lewis at the top of his voice.

"Way hayeeeeee."

His voice echoed, and the wind snatched it and threw it in ribbons round my ears, and it was then I knew for certain what I'd always suspected — he was a bleeding nutter, Spike Lewis.

'Course he was. He was right off his beanpole.

I'd never have mitched off school today but for him.

I'd never have been had up for nicking lead down Bute Terrace.

I'd never have seen my dad's tears and the long, slow look of pain in my mam's eyes.

"This is the bleeding life," screamed Spike Lewis, and he

stood up in the bow and raised his arms to the heavens.

"Sit down, you madman, you'll have the bloody boat over," shouted Soapy Rodgers. "Sit down, mun."

Spike Lewis turned. Very slowly.

"Scared, is it, Soapy?" he said.

Soapy Rodgers didn't answer.

"Lost your bottle, is it, Soapy?" he said, and this time there was barbs of anger in his voice.

Very softly Soapy Rodgers began to cry.

It was a soapy sort of cry. Like as though you was slowly squeezing out a pair of soapy football knicks into a tin drum.

"He's scared. Cor blimey, he's bleeding scared," screamed Spike Lewis.

And he began to laugh, and he began to rock the boat with his two hands tight to the gunwhales or whatever they calls the bleeding things.

And, by God, the boat didn't half rock.

It pitched and tossed, too.

And Spike Lewis began to cackle like a maniac as he turned his face to the wind and let it whip through his spikey hair.

We were well out into the estuary now.

There was fireworks sparking over Penarth.

The wind howled and the waves roared, and it was biting cold.

"Spike," I shouted.

He turned.

"What?" he said.

"Turn back, is it?" I said.

He crawled along the bottom of the boat towards me. Well, it was so rough he couldn't have kept his balance. He'd have been bleeding overboard, if he'd stood up. He hauled himself up alongside me, and he put his ear close to my mouth.

"What's that you said, my old sweetheart?" he said.

I paused.

I knew what I should say.

I didn't though.

It was what I should have said the night we broke into that house down Cathedral Road.

It was what I should have said that Saturday afternoon before we ripped the bog apart on the train to Bristol City.

It was what I should have said before we smashed into the headmaster's study and set alight to the books on his shelves.

Smashing books, they was. He'd lent me a couple. I'd enjoyed them, too. My mam had hummed happily round the house when she'd seen me reading them.

"Sling them in the Taff, is it?" Spike Lewis had said.

"Right," I'd said.

I had, too.

Two books with leather binding that felt nice and smelled nice.

Now with the boat plunging and plummeting and the spray scuttering over our backs I knew what I should say.

"What's that you was saying?" said Spike Lewis, and his fingers dug into my arm. "What's that you was saying, my old buttie boy?"

"Nothing, Spike," I said. "Nothing."

He tossed back his head, and he roared with laughter.

"We'll show them," he screamed. "We'll show the bastards."

And snickering and cackling he clawed his way back to the front of the boat, and Soapy Rodgers lay on the boards and slowly puked his ring up. I looked down on him and saw the water slopping round his thighs. It was a good nine or ten inches deep.

"Oh good God almighty," I whispered to myself. "Why didn't I say it? Why didn't I say Turn Back?"

And then I heard the roar.

It was a different roar from the roar of the wind.

It was a crashing roar. It echoed and thundered and rumbled.

It was an angry roar.

It was a malicious roar.

Malicious.

I learned that word from this book the English teacher lent me. It was a book about monsters and things like that and fairy bints with golden hair and snow white skin.

Well, this teacher was an old blokie, mind. He was about fifty or sixty and he lent me books all the time. He lent me a book by this blokie called Shalimar. It was a book about the sea and Chinese pirates and tea clippers and brigantines and engineers called McGregor and first mates with drunken captains locked in their cabins fighting typhoons and things like that.

And then I recognised what this roar was.

I'd read it in this book wrote by this blokie called Shalimar.

It was the roar of waves pounding against rocks.

I looked up quickly.

The moon had come up and there was stars, too.

And in the moonlight I saw it.

I saw the great cliffs of Steepholm Island and the waves crashing against them.

And the tide was sending us racing towards them.

"Soapy," I yelled. "Soapy."

He didn't move.

"Soapy, you black bastard," I bawled.

I kicked him.

I pounded him on the back with my fists.

I took him by the scruff of his neck and dragged him to his knees.

"Soapy, you black bastard," I bawled again. "Look."

I yanked his head round with one hand. I pointed with the other.

I pointed to the high cliffs of Steepholm Island looming nearer and nearer and the waves spewing up them in fountains of white and roaring and gurgling and crashing and booming.

I pointed to Spike Lewis, head hunched into his shoulders, gripping the front of the boat, staring straight ahead at the great soaring cliffs and cackling and cackling.

He turned, and he saw us cowering together, clutching each other, shivering.

"Way hay," he screamed. "Way hayeeee, boys, we'll knock the living shits out of them, eh? We'll bloody show them."

And he stood up, and he stretched out his arms wide to the cliffs, and he howled at the top of his voice:

"Out of the way, you bastards. Out of the way, if you don't want doing in."

Then I remembered this story what this blokie, Shalimar, had wrote.

It was about this barquentine what the tide was tearing towards the rocks.

The captain was drunk in his cabin, and the first mate, what had got a cleft in his chin, was fighting this bloody great Lascar, what was frozen to the wheel with panic, and suddenly this cabin boy, what come from a farm in Devon, smashed open this locker and he took out...

"The rockets," I yelled to Soapy.

"What?" he said.

And his voice was all hollow.

"The rockets, you black bastard. Where've you put the

bleeding things?"

He gawped at me, and his mouth fell open.

He looked like that nigger money box what my mam give me when I was a nipper.

"The rockets," I cried at the top of my voice.

I ripped at the buttons on his jacket.

They all come off dead easy in my hands.

Well, I bet they don't have much call for sewing on buttons in Antigua.

I ripped at his pullie and I felt the rockets nestling against his chest. I wrenched them out.

My hands was so cold I could hardly hold them.

My fingers was so numb I could hardly take the matches out of the box I had in my trousers pockets.

Thank God, I'd been smoking since the age of eight.

Well, if I hadn't, I wouldn't have been carrying matches at the age of fifteen, would I?

I tried to light them, but the box was sodden, and the wind wouldn't allow no flames to grip.

The cliffs came nearer and nearer, and the roar got louder and louder and more louder still.

I began to sob.

I bloody did.

I began to sob like a babe.

I grabbed Soapy by the collar and pulled his jacket over his head.

"What you doing, butt?" he said in his hollow voice.

I crouched inside the tent I'd made of his jacket.

There was only one match left.

Light, you bastard, light.

I scratched and I scratched against the box.

"Light, you bastard," I bellowed.

It did.

Just for an instant.

But in that moment I rammed the blue touch paper of the rocket against it, and it glowed dully and then flared into life.

I shoved Soapy away and the paper sputtered and sparked.

At that moment Spike Lewis turned round.

He saw me with the rocket held out in my outstretched hand.

He opened his mouth to shout, but before any sound came from his mouth, the rocket shrieked from my hand and hit him slap in the face.

It blew up in a cloud of sparks and gold and silver spangles, and Spike Lewis screeched.

My God, I'll never forget that screech.

It was worse by far than the thunder and the roar of the waves against the cliffs.

The whole of his head seemed to go up in flames, and his coat began to burn.

He looked like the guy they'd had on the bonfire outside the Red House when my dad and my mam took me there as a nipper.

I couldn't move.

I froze solid.

And all of a sudden something very strange happened.

Soapy dragged himself to his feet and stumbled to where Spike Lewis lay spread-eagled over the bow.

He crouched over him for a moment, and by God, I thought he was going to pray or do something religious.

But, no, he took the rocket he'd snatched from my hand, and he held it into the flames coming from Spike Lewis's jacket, and he lit it, and he held it high above his head, and it curved off into the sky and it exploded in a festoon of red and green and yellow.

If the truth be known I don't remember much else.

I do remember they hauled us aboard the tug, and this blokie what smelled of wintergreen ointment poured rum through my teeth.

Some blokie in a white uniform wheeled me in a trolley along a corridor.

My mam looked down on me as I lay in bed, and for the first time in three years there was no pain in her eyes.

About a week or so later me and Soapy Rodgers took a bus to Chepstow.

Well, besides the race track they've got a hospital for burns there.

They'd bunged Spike Lewis in it.

He'd lost the sight of his eyes and his face was a bit of mess, too.

We stopped off in a pub and had a pint or two of screech.

That's what we calls rough cider in Cardiff. Screech.

Nice name. Nice sound.

When we got to the hospital gates, I took hold of Soapy Rodgers by the sleeve and I stopped him.

"What is it, my old butt?" he said.

I paused.

I knew what I had to say.

A heron flapped slowly overhead.

A magpie cackled.

What a cackle.

"Well?" said Soapy Rodgers. "What is it?"

I looked him straight in the eyes, and I said:

"Turn back, is it?"

He looked at me for a moment, and then this great slow smile came to his great black face.

"Sure," he said. "Sure we will, you white bastard."

We turned back and before we caught the bus back to Cardiff we had another couple of pints of screech.

I likes screech, I does.

If you drinks enough, it makes you forget.

The Coll Doll

by Walter Macken

"Schol" is teased because he reads a lot and wants to study. But he's been brought up in a large, poor family in difficult times in Ireland and there's no hope of proper schooling. Worse than that, at nineteen he's just lost his job. But he does have one really happy experience — until the happiness is snatched away by a simple phrase that means so much: "go in and bring out my purse"!

The Coll Doll

I was at a loose end this Monday morning in March, see. I get up in the morning all right. I have my breakfast, ready to go to work, but there is no work to go to since I was sacked on Saturday but I haven't passed on this item of information to my father and mother. There are eleven of us in the house including them, and you have to shout all the time to make yourself heard. It was that foreman. He didn't like me. I like to be clean and well turned out. That is my own business. Even if you work in a factory you don't have to look like a coal heaver all the time. I liked clean working clothes, and I liked to keep my hair well. This was my own business.

But this fellow sneered a lot at me. "Brilliantine Boy," he would say, and "The Scabby Gent". He was a big burly fellow and I took a lot from him. I don't think he meant to be nasty. He was just a big stupid, half-human ape.

I am nineteen, so on Saturday I clonked him with a spade handle. I know I shouldn't have done this. It didn't do much damage to his skull, which is as thick as his intellect, but I had no case, and nobody wept when I got my cards.

It's hard to tell your people a thing like this. All they see is that the money coming into the house is short. They don't see that a man, even if he is only nineteen, is entitled to his dignity, and entitled to defend it.

I like my oul fella, you know. He's all right. He just works, and comes home and washes and goes out to his pub and spends the night over a few pints with his friends. He'll clout you one or maybe two, but he mainly roars at us to keep us quiet. My mother is all right too, but looking after a houseful, after giving birth to them, and losing a few on the way, doesn't give her time to sit down by the fire and talk over your frustrations. You see what I mean?

I didn't like working in factories. I got a scholarship from the primary school and went on for a few years to a secondary school, but I had to quit and go to work. The money was needed at home. There's no use giving fellows like me a scholarship if they won't give the parents a sort of scholarship too, to make up for the loss of probable wages.

So I wasn't even half educated in a way. I tried to make up for this by eating books from the County Library, but you feel you are reading without direction. Your mind is going so many places at once that it is too much for it. It is like sucking the sea through a straw, see. My pals call me Schol, and pretend to defer to my knowledge, but this is just for laughs. I know myself how limited my knowledge is, and I long for it, but at the present I see no way, no way at all. All those young ones coming up after me that have to be fed and clothed on what my father earns and what I earn, or rather what I don't earn now.

So I walked, out into the country. I thought I'd take in a bit of this nature stuff, just to pass the time. It's not done, you know. Maybe on account of the tight shoes we all wear these days. All right for show and dancing, but you rarely use them to walk, just up and down the streets of the town, and you can't call that walking.

It was a bright sunny day. The sea looked happy, grinning away in the sunbeams. The hills across the bay were misted and coloured. It was odd to be walking the promenade on a Monday morning. Just a few old ladies going to Mass in the church and elderly fellows, past working, walking dogs or sitting on the seats smoking pipes.

I felt guilty, see, uneasy. I should be at work, earning money, not strolling on the prom on a Monday morning. To hell with it. I jumped down on the sand, and threw a few stones at the sea. Farther on I got flat stones and started skimming them on the calm water, seeing how many hops I could get in. The best was eleven before the stone sank.

Then I felt that the walkers' eyes were on me, saying: What is a young fellow like that doing on the sand on a Monday morning? Why isn't he working, or emigrating? One look at me and the way I was dressed, my whole appearance, and they would know I wasn't the son of a moneyed gent.

So I went away from there, seeking loneliness; even the windows of the houses and hotels seemed like accusing eyes to me. I left the promenade and walked on the winding road that left the sea and ran up and down the hill: past small rivers and down in a hollow through a wood. I leaned on the bridge here for a little while, looking at the clear water running over washed stones. I could see a shelter in the woods there, a glade that was stabbed with sunbeams shining through the branches. I thought it might be nice to go in there and lie on the grass, and stay for ever, just listening to the sound of the water, but then a large red cow, one of these walking milk bottles, came right into the middle of the glade and dropped a card, plop, plop, plop, ruining everything, see, like life, so I laughed and left.

My shoes were hurting me now. I had to stop and wriggle my toes to ease them. I was sorry I wasn't younger, like years ago when you could go in your bare feet, until the soles became as tough as leather. That was necessity. Now young people would rather be seen dead than in their bare feet. I suppose this was progress too. Here I was, thinking like I was a hundred years old.

I saw this sandy lane, so I turned down it. It looked a lonely lane, deep cartwheel tracks on it, and dry stone walls each side of it, and it was aimed in a crooked way at the sea. This was for me. The sand was soft on the feet.

It opened out into a rock-strewn beach at the sea. There was a brave smell there, of healthy things, and seaweed. There was a sandy beach as well, and at the far end a cliff rising straight up, like the back of it was covered with a green carpet. There were sheep grazing on it. Now that's the place for me, I thought, and headed for it.

I was halfway towards it, walking on the sand, thinking: Well there's no one here but me and the birds, when a girl suddenly came from the shelter of these rocks and almost ran into me. She had been behind a rock taking off her shoes and stockings I would say, and then turned for a run on the sand.

"Oh," she said, startled. "I'm sorry."

Her feet were very small and nearly as pale as the sand.

I saw fear in her face as she looked at me. All right, I was an odd fellow to see at this time and place. What did she think I was going to do? Jump on her straight away without even an introduction and rape her? She was a nice little thing, maybe seventeen or so. That's what I say, she reminded me of one of those colleen dolls you see in boxes in shop windows. She was dark and had a round face, and wide blue eyes with thick dark lashes. She was wearing a wide skirt that was like the leaves of a melodeon,[1] a white blouse and a black cardigan affair. I took all this in. I was gong to make a snide remark, because I was angry at the fear in her face but I didn't. I said: "Sorry, miss," and

---

[1] *melodeon:* kind of accordion; the girl's skirt is pleated like the expanding part of the instrument.

walked past her without another look and headed for the cliff. I was thinking: How quick people are to look at you and assess you, from your accent and your clothes and put you into a box marked Dangerous or Inferior. Without even talking to you!

I was about five minutes getting to the top of the cliff, and I stretched myself there looking at the white clouds in the blue sky.

Maybe I just gave up and drifted off to sleep. Anyhow I heard a scream. At first I thought it was a sea bird since sometimes they can cry like children. Then I sat up and turned my head and looked down at the strand. This girl was sitting down, holding her foot, and even from here I could see the scarlet of blood against the white sand. So she cut her foot, I thought. That's fine, and I went to lay back again, but she was looking straight up at me, and I couldn't do it. I got up and ran down the cliff, leaped the fence at the end and jumped down on the sand.

Her face was white. She was holding the bloody sole of her foot with small hands, and her fingers were scarlet.

I got on my knees and took the foot in my hand. It was badly gashed. I squeezed the edges of it and closed the wound. "What happened?" I asked.

"I stood on a broken bottle," she said. "Isn't it very bad?"

She was afraid now all right, but it was different fear from the other. It would take three stitches to close it, I thought.

"It's not too bad," I said. "It looks worse than it is. One stitch should close it."

"Will I bleed to death?" she asked.

I felt like patting her head. "No, no," I said. "No fear of that. Let me lift you down to the water and we'll wash it."

I put my arms under her. She wasn't very heavy. She made no protest. I carried her to the water's edge. We left a trail of blood on the sand.

I put her down there and took a clean handkerchief, and, finding sand-free water, I washed out the wound. It was a jagged gash and it was bleeding freely, which was good. I gave her the wet handkerchief.

"Wash the blood off your hands with this," I said. She did so. She was still very pale, and she was trembling. "Have you never been cut before?" I asked.

"Oh no," she said. "Just thorn cuts."

"It's not as bad as you think it is," I said. "But we'll have to get up to the main road and try and get a lift to the hospital."

"You are awful kind," she said.

I took the handkerchief and washed it in the sea, and then I tied it very tightly around her foot. I hurt her, because she gasped, but it had to be tight. "Where are your shoes and things?" I asked.

"Behind that rock," she said, pointing. I left her and went over there. Small shoes with the stockings rolled and pushed into them. I took those and put them, one each, in my coat pocket and went back to her.

"I will have to carry you now," I said.

"Amn't I very heavy?" she asked.

I lifted her easily. "Hold on to my neck," I said. She put her arms aound my neck and it eased the burden. "I'll tell you the story of the King," I said. You know this story about a king who was a great hunter and wanted to be praised, but a female of the court said that anyone could do anything with a lot of practice. So he was annoyed and ordered the forester to kill her. The forester didn't kill her, but kept her in his house in the woods. There was an outside staircase and each day she would take a small calf, put him on her shoulders and carry him up and down these stairs. He became bigger and bigger until the calf was a great big bullock, but by dint of practice she could carry the huge beast up and down the stairs. One day the King came and saw this and learned his lesson.

"What? Am I a cow?" she asked. I laughed. Some of the paleness was leaving her face.

"No," I said. "It just shows you."

"Are you often carrying girls like this?" she asked.

"Not often," I said. "You are the first."

"You are not afraid of blood and cuts?" she asked.

"I got fourteen stitches in my right leg," I said.

"How?" she asked.

"A machine that went wrong," I said. "But that's nothing. I know a man in our street with forty-eight stitches."

"Forty-eight!" she exclaimed.

I didn't say that he got the stitches as the result of a sort of bottle party, a broken-bottle party.

"That's right," I said. "So one stitch in the sole of your foot won't seem too bad."

"Oh no," she said. "I was afraid I was going to die. Isn't that silly? Wasn't I lucky you were there?"

Listen, I want to tell you something. This was the best time of my life since the day I was born. I made her laugh. I made her forget her cut, which must be paining now. I told her funny things about my young sister and my brothers, the things they got up to. She had no sisters or brothers and I felt one with her. I was carrying her in my arms. I could feel all the softness of her, her breath on the side of my cheek, her soft hair brushing against my forehead; it wasn't those things, it was just that the two of us were one person, like, going up that road. It was like the fulfilment of a daydream, if you know what I mean. She liked me, I was just me and she was just a part of me like an arm or a leg or a heart. Do you know what I mean? I thought that all things are destined, marked out to happen just like the rising and the setting of the sun. Now I could see a reason for why I was sacked, and why I walked the lonely places looking for something, searching. And I had found it. I felt that I was walking a foot above the ground. How many times in life has that happened to you?

It stayed with me. We got a lift in the first car that passed, an oldish man with a black moustache and a bald head. She was a pretty girl, of course. I would have been waiting by the side of the road for a lift until I grew whiskers, or a tinker's van would pass by. All this didn't matter. She wanted me with her, see. She got comfort for my presence. She held on to my hand and I rested her foot on my knee.

Even at the hospital she wouldn't let me go. I had to go in with her to the room where they fix up people. I knew it well, since I was a boy. It was practically a second home for us with cuts and bruises and fellows swallowing spoons and bones and things.

I held her hand while they gave her this tetanus injection and while they stitched the cut and bandaged it. Then I said, "You wait here now until I arrange for a hackney to take you home."

"Don't be long," she said. "Please come back."

She did. She said this.

I went outside the place. Turk was just swinging away having dropped a client, so I whistled him and he came back when he heard the beryl.

"What's up, Schol?" he asked. "What's the game? I'd know your whistle a mile away."

"No backchat, cabby," I said. "Just stick around. I'm bringing out a client."

"Yeah," he said, "and who pays? Any client of yours is a free ride."

I went down to him. I had a fistful of coins.

"Take your filthy lucre out of that, Scrooge," I said.

He looked at the money. "So you can pay," he said. "All right. I'll trust you."

I went back then again to her.

Now I didn't have to carry her. She was wearing one shoe on her good foot and they had a wheelchair to bring her along the corridor and out to the steps. But I carried her from there to the hackney. Turk was so surprised that he even got his great bulk out of the car and opened the back door. I put her in the seat and got in beside her. She kept holding my hand.

"Where to, miss?" Turk asked her. I was glad to see that he could see that she was a lady and treated her with respect. Otherwise he would have said something coarse. She told him where to go.

She was looking at me.

"It's all over now," I said. "It wasn't too bad, eh?"

"No," she said. "How will I ever thank you for all you have done for me?"

I didn't know how to answer that. I just swallowed my adam's apple. I don't do that often. You see, ever since it had happened, all that time she was so close to me, I had felt no evil in me. Do you know what I mean? It was all part of the clean and beautiful things of life. I know this sounds odd, blood and gaping cuts and hospitals and disinfectant, but it was so. And it wasn't just a dream, either. It was as real as life.

It seemed to me a very short time before the car went in through open iron gates and up a short winding drive. There was a house with steps leading up to it, a fine big house with lots of windows. I took her out of the car and carried her up the steps to the door. And this burst open and a very well-dressed white-haired woman came out and a maid with a black dress and a small white apron.

And the woman said: "My God! What happened? What in the name of God happened to you?"

And the girl said: "I was on the beach and I cut my foot on a bottle and he was marvellous to me. He got me to the hospital and brought me home."

"My dear! My dear!" said her mother, taking and embracing her, and then looking at me over her shoulder. Looking at me up and down, she said: "We are very grateful to you. Julia, go in and bring out my purse."

The girl said in horror: "Mother!" but it was too late, see, the bubble was burst.

I still had her other shoe and stocking in my pocket. I took it out and put it in the mother's hand, and then I turned and went down the steps and into the car beside Turk, and shouted at him: "Get out of here!" and he shifted gears and left.

I could hear voices saying: "No! No! Come back! Please come back!" but what was the use? The blindfold was down. I saw myself in her mother's eyes. Reach for the purse. A cobweb can be shattered by a stick, a big one, totally destroyed, and the spider can come along afterwards and fix it. But we are not spiders. We may be very dumb but we can see a thing when it is in front of our nose. I felt as if I had suffered a bad beating. I had been beaten before in fights, but never knocked out. I was like that now, as if I was knocked out, see.

I don't remember much after that.

We were in a pub. It was late, I think. Other men were there and Turk. And I heard Turk talking. He was saying about Schol having a doll down on the beach, a real doll, Turk's coll doll, a real smashing doll, and what he wanted to know was had Schol tumbled her on the sand.

So I hit him. And Turk hit me, and somebody else hit me, and I hit him. And later the blues were there and I hit them and they hit me with a truncheon. I fought and struck out.

Now I know I am in the lazer in the back of the police place. I am not drunk. I am sick. But I am not sick in the way that they think. I am heart sick, heart sick. So I take this stool and I start banging the door with it, so that maybe they will have to come and quieten me some more. This is what I want. Because I can tell nobody, see. It will be with me for ever. It could never be, unless I was born different and she was born different. But I can't forget, and I feel a fire eating away at my chest. And there is nobody I can tell. Nobody at all. Nobody in the wide world. Who would understand? Who would know? Who would believe?

Mort

by John Wain

*Mike finds himself having to entertain Fiona in his parents'
garden. Does she know or care what a devastating effect she has
on him? He has nothing to offer her, and the small desperate gift
he gives her means he has to disappoint someone who needs
his friendship.*

Mort

All this happened two years ago, when I was sixteen. But I still remember it quite well.

I was sitting with Mort one afternoon. I often used to drop round and see Mort, in that den of his at the top of the house. His parents had sat down and thought of everything he might possibly need, for his hobbies and having friends in. He had his books and his albums and his tapes and his photographs and slides. A little portable tv set standing on a table. A globe. His old man had even had the builders in to enlarge the window and make the room pleasant and sunny for him. Their reasoning was that if he had everything he needed up there, he'd be less likely to be always clambering up and down the stairs, putting himself at risk.

Mort was fourteen. He had this awful disease, I forget the scientific name for it, where your bones are as soft as chalk. If he moved quickly across the room and bumped against the table or something, the kind of knock you or I wouldn't even *feel*, he broke a bone. Every single time. Sometimes he broke his bones just turning over in bed. He was always having to be plastered up. And remember when Mort broke a bone, though it was so easily done, it *hurt* just as much as if you or I broke one.

Poor old Mort. I used to feel so damn sorry for him. Walking back home from his house, I don't know why I didn't burst out crying sometimes. Why did it have to happen to him, I used to think, why, why, why? He was so gentle. He had nothing but gentleness in him.

On this particular afternoon we'd been watching a football match on his little tv. I was beginning to get football out of my system, I wasn't obsessed with it like when I was twelve, but I watched a game now and then with Mort. He was pretty keen.

The match ended and he moved across the room with that slow, careful walk he'd trained himself into. A shaft of sunlight came into the room and when he turned to look at me he was standing full in it. He had this very, very fair colouring, extremely pale skin and hair so fair it was almost white, and as the sunlight shone on him I had the fancy that he looked like a boy made of paper and chalk. Paper outside, and inside, those chalky bones.

Mort was talking about the match, but I couldn't get my mind on to what he was saying. It was too full of thoughts that had come to me as we watched.

"Look, Mort," I said, interrupting him. I couldn't keep it back. "When you watch football on tv, how does it make you feel?"

"Feel?" he said. "I like to watch it if it's a good game, naturally. You get some pretty crappy stuff, even on 'Match of the Day'."

"Yes, but I mean, how does it make you feel in yourself?"

"You mean because I can't play games?" he asked.

"Well, yes. I mean, there are these twenty-two chaps, all very fit, rushing up and down the field and slamming the ball around and you ... well ... doesn't it sort of rub it all in?"

"Oh, sometimes," said Mort. I could see he wanted to change the subject. "I mean, you just have to try to keep yourself busy and not think too much about it. It's blind people I'm sorry for."

Then he started talking about his hobbies. Photography was the one he spent the money on. He had some slides he'd taken on holiday in Devon — and he'd broken a bone in his foot even there — that he was very proud of. He showed me them on a projector. They were pretty good. Then he got his new stamp album out.

"There's hardly anything in it yet," he said. "It's about three years since I started with stamps and I've only just filled the first album I had. I don't spend any money on it, you see. The way I've got it worked out, photography costs a lot, and my dad's very good about giving me enough money for that, so I try to have one hobby I don't spend anything at all on. Just the hinges."

"And the albums," I said.

"No," he said triumphantly. "The first one I got was free with some cornflake packet tops. The new one, my uncle gave me." Then his face clouded over a bit. "It's going to take me one hell of a time to get anything in it," he said. "With not buying stamps. I just get the ones people give me off their letters. And we don't seem to know anybody abroad. I hardly ever get a foreign one."

His father worked in an insurance office or something. Stuck behind a desk all day. And they were the kind of family who never went abroad.

"That'll change, Mort," I said. "As you grow up you'll get to know more and more people, and some of them are bound to live abroad, or they'll know people that do. You'll get interesting stamps, I just know it."

"That'll be the day," he said, brightening up.

I made my mind up there and then to work at getting stamps for Mort. My father's in a boring job too, he's an industrial chemist, but at least that makes him a scientist and he does belong to one or two international things. He must get some stamps. I'd never thought about the matter before because I'm not into stamps.

Soon after that I went home.

The next morning, at breakfast, I got on to my old man.

"I'm collecting stamps, Dad," I said. "For Mort."

"Postage stamps?" he said keenly. Scientists have to get things right. I suppose he thought there was a possibility Mort might have been collecting trading stamps or excise stamps.

"If you look at a letter," I said, indicating the little pile of same by his place at the table, "you'll see that in the right-hand top corner there's a piece of coloured paper, stuck on, with a numeral on it. That's a stamp. Mort collects them."

"Don't be so rude to your father, Michael," said my mother.

"Oh, he's not being rude," said my father. "Just sarcastic. Everybody's sarcastic at that age. I was myself." He lit his pipe.

He said nothing more about stamps and I thought he hadn't taken it in, but before he set out for work he went into his study and called me to join him.

"These are all the letters I've had in the last couple of months," he said, handing me a cardboard box. "I've dealt with them and I was just going to throw the envelopes away. You might find some stamps on them. Throw them away when you've finished."

I thanked him, non-sarcastically, and started looking through the envelopes. There were about fifty of them and the first forty was absolute duds. I was beginning to think there was going to be nothing for old Mort, but suddenly! Wow!

An invitation to attend some kind of conference had come to my old man from *South Korea*. Six stamps on it. Four were the same and the other two, though the same as one another, were different from the first four. They had nice sharp pictures on them of birds and flowers, and Eastern writing, as well as "Republic of Korea" in our kind of writing. I sprang to the telephone.

"Hey, Mort," I said. "You remember we were talking about stamps and you said you didn't get many?"

"Yes," he said, "what with not spending any money and not knowing anybody."

"Well, your luck's changed," I said, "now you've got me working as your agent. I've got a scoop for you already. Six stamps and guess where from? I'll give you a clue — it's in the East."

"China?" he said. "Japan?"

"South Korea," I said. I knew he'd go straight and find it, on his globe. "The Republic of South Korea."

"Magic," Mort breathed down the telephone. "When can I have them?"

"I'll drop by," I said.

I had things to do in town that morning, and it was nearly one o'clock when I got home. I found my father in the living room with a man I had never seen before. They were deep in conversation.

"This is Michael, our elder son," said my old man. "Michael, I want you to meet Professor Saltonstall. He's come over from Nottingham for this conference tomorrow."

I made the polite noises. I hadn't heard of any conference but these scientists are always having them. They don't seem able to work without looking over one another's shoulders. About Professor Saltonstall I don't remember anything except a thin, sun-browned face, round eyes behind granny-glasses, and a head bald on top, where it was likewise brown.

"My daughter's outside," he said. "She came along for the trip."

My father nodded, and the two of them looked at me expectantly, as if they had just lit a fuse and were waiting for me to go off bang. "She's in the garden," my father said.

"Does she need anything in the garden?" I asked.

"Just company, I think," said this Saltonstall and they both giggled. I suppose they would have said they chuckled, but the way it fell on my ears, they giggled.

Obviously I was expected to go out into the garden and find Miss Saltonstall, so I went out. That year we had a hammock slung between two old apple trees, and she was lying in it, reading a magazine. As I came closer I saw immediately why the two old boys had giggled. It was pure nervousness at leaving this Koh-i-noor diamond lying about without even a plain-clothes man to look after it. I was to be the plain-clothes man, evidently.

Her eyes were round like her father's but much, much bigger. Her hair was red-gold, and came down in two wings that framed her face. The arm I could see, lying across her chest, was slender and beautiful. She held up the magazine in the other hand and I saw that her nails were painted silver. Her skin was brown like her dad's — it turned out that the whole family had just got back from a holiday in Turkey or wherever the in-crowd were going that year.

I stopped in my tracks and said, "Uh, hello. I'm Mike. I expect they told you I exist."

She looked up and said, "Oh, yes." It wasn't much but it was a beginning.

Then she tried to sit up in the hammock. Actually you can't sit up in a hammock. You can jack-knife forward and sway about, but basically you have to choose between getting out of the thing altogether and just lying back. She lay back.

It came to me that happiness would be to lie in the hammock with her.

"They tell me you've come along for the trip," I said.

"Well, I'm not going to the conference, if that's what you mean," she said. I supposed she was joking but she didn't smile. "It's only today and tomorrow anyway. We're just staying two nights. Anything to get away from home for a bit of a change."

"Is there ... would you ..." I said. "Uh, is there anything you'd like to do while you're ..."

"Michael," my mother called from the French windows. "I need some help, dear. We're all having lunch in the garden."

We have no domestic help. On the other hand we have a washing-up machine, called Michael, and a chair-carrying and table-laying machine also called Michael.

"Oh, God," said the girl, trying to sit up in the hammock again. "I didn't know we were staying for lunch. I'd better go wash."

"It's hard to get out of that thing. I'll help you," I wheezed and I moved forward and held the sides of the hammock to steady it. That meant I had to lean forward across her, almost close enough to feel her body warmth. She put one hand on my shoulder as she lightly jumped down and the electric thrill went right down to the soles of my feet. When I moved I expected to see scorch marks on the grass the shape and size of my footsoles.

She landed on the grass and I backed off and looked at her as she stood there, smoothing herself down as women do. She had on a set of those farmer's overalls, or boiler-suit or whatever they call them — that bib-and-brace job. Hers were pale blue with thin stripes. Nowadays, when all the girls wear them, they mostly look as if they were all ready to begin a day's work on the farm, but she didn't. You could tell that working on a farm, even for a *minute*, was something she would never, never do.

Was I in love with her? Yes, I was already asking myself that, though our acquaintance could hardly be said to have ripened yet. No, I decided: it would be more accurate to say that I was in sex with her. What I didn't know then, because after all it was a long time ago and I was pretty inexperienced, was that it doesn't matter much what point you start from, you end up in pretty much the same mess.

"I'll show you where the bathroom is," I said, frisking around on my invisible paws and wagging my invisible tail.

"I know already," she said and went into the house.

Lunch was good. My mother slings a nice cold chicken and salad, and there was chilled white wine. I was given one glass because I was sixteen and it was a stage in my growing up. The girl had a glass too, but I noticed she didn't finish it. She put it to her lips now and then, but as if she wanted something to do with her hands. She looked a rum-and-coke type, not a wine type. She also looked pretty bored most of the time. I couldn't have blamed her, the conversation *was* boring, but I had the impression that her boredom was built-in, so to speak.

My dad and old Saltonstall talked about the conference all through lunch, and as soon as it was eaten they scampered off to go to a preliminary meeting. Under my mother's hawk-eye, I carried the dishes in and stacked them up in the kitchen.

"Aren't you going to wash them?" she asked.

"Later," I said. "I have to attend to Miss Saltonstall. She's out in the garden with no one to keep her company."

"Has she asked you to keep her company?"

"Look, it's *hospitality*," I said. "The girl's on her own in a strange town, how would you like it?" And I got out before she could stop me.

That was all right, but now came the hard part. As I walked

out into the garden I faced the fact that I had made zero progress all through lunch. All I had gathered was that the girl's name was Fiona, and even that was only because it was what her father called her. She hadn't once looked in my direction or seemed to hear the few remarks I managed to put in.

I knew, even at this stage before anything remotely describable as action had started, that in trying to get on to terms with a girl like this I was boxing out of my weight and that unless the referee stopped the fight I was going to get killed. So why was I doing it? Well, why have you done all the silly things you've done in *your* life?

So I walked over. She wasn't lying in the hammock now, she was strolling aimlessly around on the lawn. As I approached she met me with the same breathless interest she would have shown in the garden wheelbarrow.

"Hello," I said.

"Hello," she said, looking down at one elegant canvas shoe.

"Is there anything you'd ... like to do this afternoon?" I said. "I mean, I'm at a loose end ..."

It must have been obvious that I'd have said I was at a loose end even if I had in fact fixed up to have an audience with the Pope, followed by a front seat at the Cup Final and dinner with Goldie Hawn. I didn't exactly get down on my hands and knees and lick her hand, but if she had put out a tin of Pedigree Chum I would have got down and slurped it up without using my hands.

"Do?" she said as if it didn't matter much. "We could go for a drive somewhere, if your father isn't using the car."

"I don't drive," I said. "I'm not old enough for a licence yet."

She almost yawned in my face. I suppose the blokes who normally took her out all had cars and buzzed her around anywhere she felt inclined to buzz. Well, I would have a car, soon. I would leave school and get into some racket that made money and I would have a De Tomaso Pantero, with a silver cigarette lighter and ocelot-skin seat covers.

"Well, I don't suppose there's anything *else* to do," she said.

"We could go for a walk."

"A walk? Whatever for?"

"I could, uh, show you the nice parts of town."

"I'll go to the shops later," she said. "There's probably a bus that goes there."

"Oh, yes," I said, wagging my tail and leaping up and down

till my identity disc jangled at my throat. "You can take a number 2, that goes straight to where all the main shops are, or you can take a 2A or a 2B, they turn off just before you get to $-$"

"All right. You'd better show me where the stop is."

"I could come with you," I said. "I know where all the boutiques and things are." I didn't. "And I could help to carry anything heavy."

"I'm not buying a *piano*, for God's sake. I'm just looking round. I might not buy anything at all."

"Well, I'll show you where the bus goes from," I said.

There was a silence. It was the dead time of the afternoon. Insects hummed around, but the rest of creation was in stupor. I tried to flog my brain into thinking of something to say, but I couldn't. The trouble is, I can talk best to people I like, and although I knew I loved Fiona and always would love her, I didn't like her very much.

"What do you do?" I finally forced out. My voice sounded harsh and abrupt, as if I were giving her some sort of security grilling.

"Do? I don't do anything."

"Well, but I mean ... when you get up in the morning, what do you do till you go to bed at night?"

"I'm at school," she said as if that closed the whole discussion — as I'm sure it did, for her.

We sat there in the insect-humming emptiness again until finally I said, "School can't last for ever. What will you do afterwards?"

"I know what I'd *like* to do," she said. "Be an actress."

"Oh," I said. "Will you go to drama school?"

She laughed, musically. Her laugh sounded like condensed milk being poured over a xylophone. I liked it.

"God, no," she said. "They teach you all that boring theatre stuff. I want to be a television actress."

I saw it. Millions of people seeing you every time you went on the box, your face being recognised everywhere, men drooling over you in railway carriages. I loved her more and more, but God, how I hated the kind of thoughts that went on in her mind.

"What television actresses d'you like?" she asked me suddenly, turning to look me straight in the face for about the first time. I knew it was just market research, that she'd have asked the same question of any OAP she found herself sitting next to on the bus, but I wanted to answer anyway. I tried to think of some trendy name that would impress her.

But the best I could come up with was, "Gayle Hunnicut."

"Oh, come on," she said. "I mean someone closer to my *generation*. I was thinking of people like Joanna Lumley. Or Rula Lenska."

"Oh," I said. "I see. Yes." I was a square, out of touch, a peasant, a backwoods type just in from the tall rhubarbs.

"I might as well go to the shops now," Fiona said. She went over to the hammock and collected some odds and ends: a purse, a pair of sunglasses. These latter she put on, perching them on the top of her head. That was as near as I saw them come to her eyes, but the effect was good. Always, whatever she did, the effect would be good.

We set off to walk to the bus stop. It was about eight minutes' walk away. That gave me $8 + x$ minutes of her company, where x was the number of minutes it took the bus to arrive. Normally you had to wait anything up to ninety-six hours at that bus stop, but I wouldn't have minded betting that this time a bus would draw up at the exact second we got there.

Then, as we went down the garden path, I had a brainwave.

"I expect you like dancing," I said.

"Pretty much. Depends if it's fun."

"Well," I babbled, "there's a disco tonight. At my school. It's for the Sixth Form. I'd like to take you if you're ... not doing anything. It's pretty exclusive but I'm sure you'll be welcome."

Welcome to me, anyway. Actually by taking someone from outside I'd be breaking a pretty hefty unwritten rule, but short of getting actually thrown out I didn't care.

"I don't mind going to a disco," she said. "Thanks. What time do we have to be there?"

"If you'll tell me where you're staying," I said, "I'll pick you up." In my De Tomaso, with reclining front seats. "It's all right if we get there any time after half past seven."

"Half past seven? That's pretty early; isn't it?"

"Well, we have to start a bit early. They get stroppy as hell if we're not finished and the lights out by eleven."

She didn't say anything but her face said it all. Eleven!

"I think you'll enjoy it," I said.

She gave a little shrug as she walked along. "I'll give it a whirl anyway. Thanks."

I felt more confident now and we still had five minutes to go before reaching the bus stop, not to mention any x minutes I might be granted by fate. I had a sudden rush of confidence.

"So, what else are you interested in? Besides being an actress?"

"Oh, just the usual things."

"Like what?"

"We're full of questions, aren't we?" she said. "What is this, the third degree? You're like my *parents*, for God's sake."

"No, I'm not," I said. "I'm not like your parents at all, Fiona." Using her name sent a shock-wave right through me. "I'm just trying to find out what you're interested in because we're going to spend some time together."

"Well, you don't get much time to discuss your hobbies at a disco. I don't think you'll need to know much about my interests. Anyway I haven't got any."

"You're not interested in *anything*?"

"I *told* you, *no*."

I had to keep talking. The bus stop was just round the next corner. "Do you *collect* anything?"

"Collect anything? No. Yes. I collect some things."

"What sort of things?"

"Oh, God. China boxes. Victorian buttons. Stamps."

"Stamps!" I said, stopping short. She just kept walking on, and I had to accelerate to catch up with her. "You collect stamps?"

"Yes," she said, looking straight in front of her.

"I'm glad you mentioned it," I said. She hadn't mentioned it. I had bayoneted it out of her. "I get some pretty interesting stamps. My father belongs to a lot of international companies and things. I get a lot of foreign stamps from him. I don't collect them myself so I give them away."

"Well, I'll have some if they're going spare," she said.

"Going spare — I should just say they are. Only this morning I got six Korean stamps off the one envelope. Republic of South Korea — six of them. They're pretty rare."

"Here's the bus," she said. It came swishing up just as we got to the stop. How had I known it would do that?

The disco was dark and loud. She had changed out of her farmer's overalls and now she was wearing a check shirt and a pair of black jeans that fitted so closely they looked as if they had been sprayed on. I imagined her trying to get them off at night. I thought she would have to shred them away with a knife, like the brown skin of an onion. Her hair was different too. Instead of coming down on either side of her face, it was drawn back and hung down in a ponytail. When she swayed her body to the music, her red-gold ponytail swung gracefully from side to side.

We didn't exchange more than fifty words the whole evening, and that was mostly when I asked her what she would like from the soft drinks bar, things like that. The bar was manned, or rather girled, by some of my dearly beloved fellow-Sixth Formers, and I had to put up with some looks of the kind I believe they call "quizzical". I took no notice. I just wanted to grab something in a plastic mug and get back with it to Fiona.

We didn't talk, as I say, but she seemed to like the music and I thought on the whole she was enjoying herself. Just the noise, and the darkness and coloured lights, and the rhythm, and the presence of all those young males, seemed to work on her. At least that's the only explanation I can give of what happened next.

About two-thirds of the way through the evening she suddenly put her mouth close to my ear (it was the only way to be heard) and said, "Let's go outside."

We were both so hot we were practically sizzling, so I assumed she just wanted the cool night breeze. And probably that was the reason, or most of it. But this is what happened. We went out of the building and across to the playing field, which was lined with trees. The leaves of the trees gently stirred over our heads, though there was no breeze that you could feel on your skin; the school was built on a hill, and you could see the lights of the town below, with the main roads picked out in necklaces of yellow drops. It was all very romantic. And she leaned her back against the rough trunk of a tree and pulled me towards her and kissed me.

That's all. Nothing else happened. Nothing else *could* happen; it was the final cataclysm, the earthquake that ended one part of my life and started another. The kiss wasn't a very long one, and by comparison with some of the ones I've had since I daresay it was amateurish, because I'm a lot older now and I get around to an extent. But it was the best I shall ever have in my life.

I tried to get another one as we were walking home. I took hold of her and gently tried to pull her towards me, but she just kept walking straight ahead.

So I did the only thing left that I could do. I took out my wallet and produced the six Korean stamps. I'd cut them off the envelope, very carefully, and brought them with me in case they helped the evening along. Now, I was glad I had.

"I've got something for you," I said.

"What's that then?" she said, not very interested, but not very bored either.

"Those stamps I was talking about," I said. "The Korean ones. All six." And I handed them over.

"Well, thanks," she said. "It was nice of you to remember."

Her check shirt had a button-down pocket over each breast. She unbuttoned the right-hand one and put the stamps carefully inside. I had a wild urge to help her to fasten it up again, but she managed without me. I thought of the stamps nestling against her right nipple, and I swear I nearly fainted away.

Then we walked back to where she was staying and she went in. I walked on home; at least I have to assume I did, though when I got there I didn't remember walking the last ten minutes.

So there I was, on the telephone, about a week after Fiona went back. I heard it ringing in their house. I'd winkled old Saltonstall's home telephone number out of my father, and as it rang I decided that if he answered it, or if anybody answered it whose voice I didn't recognise, I'd hang up and go and shoot myself.

I was just thinking this when the ringing stopped and a high, young female voice said, "Hello?"

"Fiona?"

"Fiona's out," said the voice and gave a little breathless giggle. Fiona hadn't told me she had a younger sister, but then she hadn't told me *anything*.

"But she's at home at present, isn't she, I mean ..."

"She's out." Giggle.

"Yes, she's out at the moment, all right, but she's basically at home, she's not away on holiday or anything?"

I'm one of those people who have to form a picture of anyone they're talking to on the telephone. I pictured this younger sister as a skinny kid, soon to be beautiful like Fiona the pacesetter, but just now with freckles and pigtails and perhaps braces.

"When will Fiona be in?" I asked. There was the sound of a minor scuffle at the other end, and muttering. I could tell someone else was taking over. Then a woman's voice said, "Can I help you? Who is it, please?"

The first voice had been a young, silly version of Fiona's. This was an old, sensible version. Her mum.

I said who I was. It didn't mean anything to her so I said, "When Professor Saltonstall came over for that conference, he brought Fiona with him."

An electronic voice in my head started sounding the syllables *Fee Own a Salt On Stall, Fee Own a Salt on Stall,* meaninglessly.

"Oh, *yes.* You're Michael. Of course I remember now."

Had she mentioned me? Or was it just family small talk?

"My husband said how kind you all were, and hospitable." She sounded a very nice woman.

"Oh," I said. "Good. I mean, it was nothing. It was a pleasure, I mean. Well, look, what I was ringing about ..."

What was I ringing about? My mind had gone blank. Oh, yes, my decision to hitch-hike to Nottingham and catch another glimpse of *Fee Own a.* "I shall be in Nottingham next weekend and I just wondered ..."

"How nice. Well, do come and visit us."

I nodded, just as if she could see me.

"I don't know what Fiona's plans are. I suppose it's her you want to see, isn't it, mostly?" Good thinking, madam. "Is it Saturday or Sunday you'll be in Nottingham?"

"Saturday," I said. "Or Sunday. It could be either one, actually. I mean, I've no ..."

"Well, Sunday's no good because we're going out for the day. So let's say Saturday. I don't know what Fiona's plans are, but she's bound to be in some of the time. Let's put it this way. If you turn up here on Saturday we'll be very glad to see you, Michael, and we'll give you a meal if you want one."

I thanked her. It was pretty nice of her, especially considering the number of blokes she must have hanging about, leaving trails of saliva along the garden path. Then I hung up.

I set out on Saturday morning. It took me hell's own time to get to Nottingham — it's over a hundred miles and I'm not good at hitch-hiking. I get on to the wrong traffic arteries. I went and stood by the main road at half past eight in the morning and it was nearly three by the time I got to Nottingham. Then it took me another long time to get to the Saltonstall homestead, about two hundred miles out of town. Finally I got there and the kid sister answered the door. I had imagined her all wrong. She had a round face and a dark brown crew-cut, no freckles, and her teeth were all right.

She said she was the only person at home. When I asked when the others might be back she disclaimed all knowledge. She seemed to be trying to convey that they had gone on a voyage up the Orinoco or something.

I said I'd wait in the garden. There was a deck chair on the lawn and I sat down in it and tried to keep from thinking. The attempt was a complete failure. I thought about Fiona, I thought what a bloody fool I was making of myself, I thought how I had watched my father's mail for some more stamps to bring her and hadn't found any. That made me think of Mort, and I pictured him looking at his globe to find South Korea. But I stopped that. I pulled my mind on to something else. Fiona's ponytail.

Then the mother came home. She was just as nice as she had seemed on the telephone. But Fiona got her looks from her father, I could see that. The mother was brown-haired and rather round faced, like the younger daughter, I liked her a lot. She made me a huge sandwich with about six layers to it, and sat with me in the kitchen while I ate it.

Then Fiona came in. She was carrying a tennis racquet but she wasn't wearing tennis clothes. She was wearing a denim skirt, and sandals.

"Hello," she said to me. "Can we eat early tonight, Mother? I have to go out."

"Michael's come a long way to see you, dear," her mother said.

"Oh yes," Fiona said. She put the tennis racquet on the table.

"Not there, dear," said her mother. "In the games cupboard."

"How did you get here?" Fiona asked me.

"I hitched."

"Why don't you go out and sit in the garden?" said her mother, letting it ride about the tennis racquet.

We went out but we didn't sit down. We walked around the lawn for a bit. Fiona had only been with me two minutes but I could seee she was already waiting for me to go.

"I hope you enjoyed your visit to our part of the world," I said.

"Oh, yes."

"The disco was fun, wasn't it?"

"Yes. I always enjoy a disco."

And you always give a kiss to whoever takes you. You lean

your back against a tree, or perhaps a wall, and you kiss him.

"I, uh, couldn't get any more stamps just yet," I said. "I've been looking out, but, well, they just haven't..."

"Stamps?"

"Yes. You collect them. I gave you those six from Korea. I expect you've got them in your album by now."

"I haven't got an album," Fiona said. She turned and looked straight in my face with a this-has-gone-far-enough expression. "I don't remember telling you I was a stamp collector."

"Well, you did," I said. "You told me when I was walking you to the bus stop and then I gave you those six Korean stamps when we were coming home from the disco. You seemed quite glad to have them."

"Yes, I was glad to have them." She had stopped walking now and just stood still, looking at me like a landowner who's caught someone trespassing. "I'm always glad to have anything that might be worth a bit of money."

"Oh yes," I said. "Money."

"I always accept anything people give me and then I try to sell it. I'm sorry if that shocks you. I'm always short of money because clothes cost so much."

"I'm sure they do," I said.

"Never once, never one single day of my life," said Fiona, speaking at dictation speed to make sure it sank in, "have I had enough money to buy the clothes I want. The kind of career I want to have, it's going to depend on being in the right places and being seen by the right people and *looking good*."

"I'm sure you'll do all those things."

"I have to go about in *rags*," she said, glancing down at her denim skirt, "and I'm always way behind the fashion."

"That's the fashion's problem, not yours," I said. I suddenly felt calm. It was all so hopeless. I just relaxed. There was no point in getting excited over Fiona any more. There was no point in getting excited over *anything* any more, for the rest of my life.

"I'll do anything to try to get a bit of cash together. I thought if those stamps were rare I might take them to a shop or somewhere and get a bit for them, if it was only something like fifty pence. That's how hard-up I am."

"And did you?" I asked.

"No. Even *that* went wrong. I had them in my shirt pocket and I forgot to take them out and my mother put the shirt through the washing machine and then the dryer. They were just stiff crumpled bits of paper at the end of it so I threw them away."

"Oh," I said. "I'm sorry. You might have been able to sell them."

Then I was outside the garden gate with my face towards the main road. As I walked away I turned round just once, the kid sister was watching me from an upstairs window, and Fiona had gone into the house.

The next afternoon I went round to see Mort. I reckoned I might as well get it over. His mother told me he was in his room so I went straight up. What she didn't tell me was that he had broken another bone. His left forearm was plastered up and had a sling.

"I did it just yesterday," he told me.

"I'm really sorry, Mort."

"Oh, it isn't so serious," he said. "Just a small bone in my wrist. It doesn't hurt much. Did you see that ice hockey on tv last night? Those two Canadian teams?"

"No," I said.

"Sensational," he said. "The body-checking...wow!"

"Ice hockey's quite a game," I said. "Look, Mort. I've got some bad news."

"It's about the stamps, isn't it?" he said.

"How d'you know?"

"Because you haven't given them to me yet," he said. "If you were going to, it would have been the first thing you mentioned. You'd have had them in your hand as you came through the door because you're like that."

"Well, look, Mort, you might as well know, the stamps got destroyed," I said. That much at least was true, now for the lies. "I didn't cut them off the envelope, I thought you might have fun doing that, and I left the envelope on the work table in my room. It was lying with a bunch of old envelopes and our cleaning woman picked the whole lot up and threw them away."

We have no cleaning woman. We clean the house ourselves, when we get round to it.

"Where did she throw them to?" Mort asked.

"She burnt them. She always burns the waste paper in the garden incinerator. She ought to send it to be recycled but she never does."

"Well," Mort said, "it would have been a waste to recycle Korean stamps. I'd rather think of them being burnt, somehow."

"I'm sorry, Mort," I said.

"It's not your fault," he said. His stamp album, I now saw, was open on the table and I would have taken a bet, though I didn't look, that it was open at K. "It was nice of you anyway."

"What was nice of me?"

"To want to give me the stamps," he said.

I was silent, then said, "I hope your wrist doesn't hurt too much."

"Oh, not too much," he said. "It aches but I'll get used to it."

Then I told Mort I had an appointment at the dentist's. I went home and spent the afternoon in the hammock, spreading my limbs out as if I'd never walk again, lying where Fiona had lain.

Meeting in Milkmarket

by John Wickham

Stanley is an adult now, but has always remembered his brief friendship in a Barbadian elementary school with George. Now the two meet again, in a street in Barbados, the Milkmarket.

Meeting in Milkmarket

Thirty-five years ago George Sampeter and I sat in the same class next to each other in the elementary school. We were friends, by which I mean that he was easy with me and I liked him and was easy with him. You will see that I am using "friends" in the sense in which I would have used it as a child, innocently and trustingly. Now, before I use the word, I must, as it were, look behind my back. I must ask myself whether the thing that exists deserves the name, whether I am not perhaps claiming too much. But I was less cautious when George and I walked together from school and shared sugar cakes and fish cakes and I did not question whether the thing that we shared could justify its claim to the title of friendship.

Today I met George in the Milkmarket after more than thirty years. The thing that strikes me now is my own reaction to meeting him after so long. From day to day I often see men who went to school with me and who have, in the common way of speaking, done well for themselves. They are now doctors and lawyers, some of them, politicians and high-up civil servants and one of them is the chief justice, a knight and counsel of the queen. Sometimes, depending on the propitiousness of the occasion, the time of day or night, the place and the surroundings, the degree of sobriety, they see me too and nod a greeting or avert their eyes to a shop window as the case may be. Whenever I encounter one of these people I always feel a burning angry shame and self-contempt and invariably that day or night I contrive to get quite drunk. Nowadays I get drunk much too often. They know not what they do, these people. And this is why I am not afraid to say that George was my friend, is my friend, for seeing him has left me happy and glad in a choking way that I was at school with him, glad for myself and somehow simply and unambiguously rewarded by the memory that when we were children I shared in his life and experiences.

I remember very clearly the morning that George came to school for the first time. He was late and prayers had already been said when his father led him through the schoolroom to the headmaster's desk on the platform. I could see that he was frightened by the way he held on to his father's hand and I felt a trifle sorry for him that he needed a hand to clutch for support in what seemed to me no great ordeal. I think now that there was

48

also in me a little envy of his fortune in having a father's hand to clutch. The headmaster greeted George's father warmly and it was clear that they were friends and that George would be one of those boys who would get special treatment, being the son of the head's friend. That made me angry, I remember. What made me even more angry was that George was put straight into the second standard. This seemed a monstrous piece of favouritism. But it did not last long. By the next morning George was among us humbler folk in the first standard: he could read very well and on this basis had been put into the class above but the teacher soon found out that George couldn't do sums and so, according to the rule which counted skill at sums as superior to all other skills, George had to be demoted. They put him to sit next to me. He was crying from the public shame. I wanted to comfort him but I could think of no way of doing it. He had a new slate and a new pencil which for some reason would not write. I had an old cigarette tin full of pencil ends (in all my school days I never had a whole pencil) and I gave him one and showed him how to lick the tip with his tongue to make it write. We became friends from that moment and I have never ceased to be proud of myself for that simple gesture. I have done nothing in my life since, which has pleased me more.

George came from the country and brought with him a sense of wonder and thrill at the sights of town. Our school was a slum school in the heart of the dirty back streets, littered with fruit skins, reeking with the "fainty-fainty" smell of rotten and rotting fruit. In the doorways of Suttle Street the patois-speaking mesdames from Dominica and St Lucia watched over barrels of mangoes and sacks of charcoal. All sort of spices spread a perfume in the air and the girls of the town, their mouths filled with gold and curses, slutted and strutted along the narrow wet street. George loved it all. I did not, I lived in it. After school every afternoon I would try to persuade George to take the road by way of the waterfront so that we might look at the schooners and the barebacked seamen smoking on the decks or fishing over the sides: the smell of the sea offered a more promising and certainly cleaner prospect than the one that hedged me around in Suttle Street. But the dirt and the muck fascinated George: the sacking curtains that screened the beds from the street, the smoky oil lamps, the half-starved dogs, kicked from one end of the road to the other. He would spend an hour listening to the patois shouts and curses that flew across the street and so miss his bus.

George in those days had a country boy's simplicity and lack of guile and I prided myself on my sharpness, my knowledge of the back streets and the ways of the city. I showed off to George and he rewarded me by finding everything I showed him fascinating.

My mother made our living by taking in washing and selling sugar cakes and fish cakes at the door of our house. As I have said, after school in the afternoon, I was always reluctant to take the road past our house on our way to George's bus. It is easy to say that I was ashamed and did not want George to see where I lived, but this would have been true only at first. It was more than that, I think Suttle Street was a dirty, filthy place. It was never clean. I lived there because I had no other place to live but I hated the place. But there was another reason for George's eagerness to pass by my house which I never suspected. It was my mother who told me one evening when I came home alone that she thought that he was fond of my sister Florianne. Like so many other facts, as soon as I had been told I recognised this as true beyond question and could not understand how I could have failed to see it before. George could draw very well and he was forever filling his drawing book with sketches of Florianne and asking me to give them to her. As far as I remember, he never spoke more than a few words to her when they met on the road before or after school. Florianne went to the girls' school next to the church and since this was on our way home, she had to dawdle to make sure of meeting us. Others besides my mother had noticed it too and very soon George became the victim of some very cruel teasing from the boys which led, in the end, to the end of the affair, such as it was.

I find it now very difficult to say all this. First of all, it happened such a long time ago and then, although in my memory it seems big and important and to contain the distillation of our time and place, yet I have a misgiving that it is pitiably trivial and not worth the weight which my own heart seems to give it. And yet I know that I was right and that the trivial events of thirty years ago opened my eyes to the realities. It has always amused me when people refer to sexual and biological matters as the facts of life and imply that the child who has been made aware of them is no longer to be thought of as a child. But the true facts of life are hardly so simple. The mating of male and female and the resulting production of animal life, these in my experience hold less mystery and need far less explanation than the conventions and artificialities which we have erected to separate one man from another. Yet no one explains or tries to explain these facts of life to a child who is left to blunder against closed doors, to fumble with false combinations and finally to wander forever in a bewilderment from which neither age nor future experience ever succeeds in rescuing him.

The teasing of the boys was not malicious, and yet I cannot be sure. Perhaps, after all, it was more than a simple recital of the facts and contained some recognition that any conceivable affection between George and my sister upset some sort of balance and did not fit into a desirable scheme of things. It was not that our schoolfellows were more than normally class conscious in any crude way but they reacted in the only way they knew to an incongruity which they recognised immediately. They laughed and chanted: "Georgie like a barefoot girl." They saw no irony in the fact that several of them wore no shoes themselves. They repeated the chant at every opportunity until the simple fact became a taunt, then an accusation, and then something like a savage curse. I can hear it now, the ringing almost triumphant "Georgie like a barefoot girl" as three or four boys trail behind George and myself as we turn the corner by the church and the girls' school. The words seem to tell the total story of our society. They need no explanation, they stand by themselves as a monument to the crassness of human thinking, the grossness of our sentiments and the thoughtless, awful cruelty of our behaviour.

"Georgie like a barefoot girl." The chanted refrain echoes in my memory and even now I can feel the helpless anger which flooded through me. I was helpless but George was both helpless and frightened. He had never experienced anything like it and his patent terror made me take what action I could to help him — action that showed how ignorant I was of the ways of the adult world.

One morning George came as usual to wait for me while I got myself ready for school. As he waited outside in the street while I swallowed my breakfast biscuit, four boys turned the corner by the grocery. George sensed that they would begin their usual chant and tried to escape by diving into our front room. But he could not escape and when I came out of the back room I found him cornered like an animal while the four boys chanted the usual words. My mother was not at home but Florianne was and I could hear her sobs as she tried to stifle them by burying her head in the bedclothes. George and I were followed all the way to school by the cruel refrain.

I went straight to the headmaster, thinking in my innocence that as he was the friend of George's father, he would at least find some sort of suitable rebuke for the boys. What he did was much simpler. He summoned George and told him that he must stop at once his practice of walking along Suttle Street. There were other roads, he said, decent roads which George could take. He also told George's father some version of the story for, from the following morning, someone accompanied George to school and came in the afternoon to collect him. That was the end of our walks through town, our idlings by the waterfront and the shop windows, the end of something which had hardly begun but which we had shared, the end of any promise which our friendship had seemed to hold. It was not long after that George left the elementary school and our paths ceased to cross.

Today it seems strange that in all the in-between years we never so much as spoke to each other: we might just as well have been in different worlds. I did see George some years after when he was about sixteen, playing cricket for his school. When he came to bat, my heart was in my mouth for him but he could not know that I was in the crowd. And then I heard that he had gone abroad and that was all.

Today he saw me before I saw him. His voice has not changed very much, it had always been deep. He shouted to me from the other side of the street and when I heard my name I turned to see him smiling. I was as pleased as a child, I can't say how pleased I was. He shook my hand and asked how I was. His voice was careful and controlled. I could not answer. My clothes, the shiny old trousers, spoke for themselves. He was confident, assured, in a sports shirt and light cotton slacks and open-toed sandals, like a tourist. It was good to see him and to be remembered by him. And then a cloud crossed his face and he said, "Stanley, it's been a long time, I am glad to see you, but I must run." "Yes," I said. I understood. He let go of my hand while he spoke and after he had left me I stood watching his figure mingle with the crowd in the Milkmarket.

But what I cannot understand is why, as he was leaving I should have said to him, to George, my friend, "Goodbye, sir."

The Coming of Maureen Peal

by Toni Morrison

Claudia and Frieda are sisters attending an American school. It is a very cold winter, and they are looking forward to spring. But their pleasure is spoiled by the arrival of a new girl: they are black and she is white; they are poor and she is rich. To make it worse, the new girl, Maureen Peal, charms everybody. Claudia and Frieda are very jealous — but what are they really jealous about?

The Coming of Maureen Peal

My daddy's face is a study. Winter moves into it and presides there. His eyes become a cliff of snow threatening to avalanche; his eyebrows bend like black limbs of leafless trees. His skin takes on the pale, cheerless yellow of winter sun; for a jaw he has the edges of a snowbound field dotted with stubble; his high forehead is the frozen sweep of the Erie[1], hiding currents of gelid[2] thoughts that eddy in darkness. Wolf killer turned hawk fighter, he worked night and day to keep one from the door and the other from under the windowsills. A Vulcan guarding the flames, he gives us instructions about which doors to keep closed or opened for proper distribution of heat, lays kindling by, discusses qualities of coal, and teaches us how to rake, feed, and bank the fire. And he will not unrazor his lips until spring.

Winter tightened our heads with a band of cold and melted our eyes. We put pepper in the feet of our stockings, Vaseline on our faces, and stared through dark icebox mornings at four stewed prunes, slippery lumps of oatmeal, and cocoa with a roof of skin.

But mostly we waited for spring, when there could be gardens.

By the time this winter had stiffened itself into a hateful knot that nothing could loosen, something did loosen it, or rather someone. A someone who splintered the knot into silver threads that tangled us, netted us, made us long for the dull chafe of the previous boredom.

This disrupter of seasons was a new girl in school named Maureen Peal. A high-yellow dream child with long brown hair braided into two lynch ropes that hung down her back. She was rich, at least by our standards, as rich as the richest of the white girls, swaddled in comfort and care. The quality of her clothes threatened to derange Frieda and me. Patent leather shoes with buckles, a cheaper version of which we got only at Easter and which had disintegrated by the end of May. Fluffy sweaters the colour of lemon drops tucked into skirts with pleats so orderly

---

[1] *Erie:* a large lake in the USA
[2] *gelid:* very cold indeed

they astounded us. Brightly coloured knee socks with white borders, a brown velvet coat trimmed in white rabbit fur, and a matching muff. There was a hint of spring in her sloe green eyes, something summery in her complexion, and a rich autumn ripeness in her walk.

She enchanted the entire school. When teachers called on her, they smiled encouragingly. Black boys didn't trip her in the halls[1]; white boys didn't stone her, white girls didn't suck their teeth when she was assigned to be their work partners; black girls stepped aside when she wanted to use the sink in the girl's toilet, and their eyes genuflected under sliding lids. She never had to search for anybody to eat with in the cafeteria — they flocked to the table of her choice, where she opened fastidious lunches, shaming our jelly-stained bread with egg salad sandwiches cut into four dainty squares, pink-frosted cupcakes, sticks of celery and carrots, proud, dark apples. She even bought and liked white milk.

Frieda and I were bemused, irritated, and fascinated by her. We looked hard for flaws to restore our equilibrium, but had to be content at first with uglying up her name, changing Maureen Peal to Meringue Pie. Later a minor epiphany[2] was ours when we discovered that she had a dog tooth — a charming one to be sure — but a dog tooth nonetheless. And when we found out that she had been born with six fingers on each hand and that there was a little bump where each extra one had been removed, we smiled. They were small triumphs, but we took what we could get — snickering behind her back and calling her Six-finger-dog-tooth-meringue-pie. But we had to do it alone, for none of the other girls would co-operate with our hostility. They adored her.

When she was assigned a locker next to mine, I could indulge my jealousy four times a day. My sister and I both suspected that we were secretly prepared to be her friend, if she would let us, but I knew it would be a dangerous friendship, for when my eye traced the white border patterns of those Kelly-green knee socks, and felt the pull and slack of my brown stockings, I wanted to kick her. And when I thought of the unearned haughtiness in her eyes, I plotted accidental slammings of locker doors on her hand.

As locker friends, however, we got to know each other a little,

[1] *halls:* corridors, which are very wide and have lockers in them
[2] *epiphany:* in this case, a marvellous appearance

and I was even able to hold a sensible conversation with her without visualising her fall off a cliff, or giggling my way into what I thought was a clever insult.

One day, while I waited at the locker for Frieda, she joined me.

"Hi."

"Hi."

"Waiting for your sister?"

"Uh-huh."

"Which way do you go home?"

"Down Twenty-first Street to Broadway."

"Why don't you go down Twenty-second Street?"

"'Cause I live on Twenty-first Street."

"Oh. I can walk that way, I guess. Partly, anyway."

"Free country."

Frieda came toward us, her brown stockings straining at the knees because she had tucked the toe under to hide a hole in the foot.

"Maureen's gonna walk part way with us."

Frieda and I exchanged glances, her eyes begging my restraint, mine promising nothing.

It was a false spring day, which, like Maureen, had pierced the shell of a deadening winter. There were puddles, mud, and an inviting warmth that deluded us. The kind of day on which we draped our coats over our heads, left our galoshes in school, and came down with croup the following day. We always responded to the slightest change in weather, the most minute shifts in time of day. Long before seeds were stirring, Frieda and I were scruffing and poking at the earth, swallowing air, drinking rain...

As we emerged from the school with Maureen, we began to moult immediately. We put our head scarves in our coat pockets, and our coats on our heads. I was wondering how to manoeuvre Maureen's fur muff into a gutter when a commotion in the playground distracted us. A group of boys was circling and holding at bay a victim, Pecola Breedlove.

Bay Boy, Woodrow Cain, Buddy Wilson, Junie Bug — like a necklace of semi-precious stones they surrounded her. Heady with the smell of their own musk, thrilled by the easy power of a majority, they gaily harassed her.

"Black e mo. Black e mo. Yadaddsleepsnekked. Black e mo black e mo ya dadd sleeps nekked. Black e mo ..."

They had extemporised a verse made up of two insults about matters over which the victim had no control; the colour of her skin and speculations on the sleeping habits of an adult, wildly fitting in its incoherence. That they themselves were black, or that their own father had similarly relaxed habits was irrelevant. It was their contempt for their own blackness that gave the first insult its teeth. They seemed to have taken all of their smoothly cultivated ignorance, their exquisitely learned self-hatred, their elaborately designed hopelessness and sucked it all up into a fiery cone of scorn that had burned for ages in the hollows of their minds − cooled − and spilled over lips of outrage, consuming whatever was in its path. They danced a macabre ballet around the victim, whom, for their own sake, they were prepared to sacrifice to the flaming pit.

Black e mo Black e mo Ya daddy sleeps nekked.
Stch ta ta stch ta ta
stach ta ta ta ta ta

Pecola edged around the circle crying. She had dropped her notebook, and covered her eyes with her hands.

We watched, afraid they might notice us and turn their energies our way. Then Frieda, with set lips and Mama's eyes, snatched her coat from her head and threw it on the ground. She ran toward them and brought her books down on Woodrow Cain's head. The circle broke. Woodrow Cain grabbed his head.

"Hey, girl!"

"You cut that out, you hear?" I had never heard Frieda's voice so loud and clear.

Maybe because Frieda was taller than he was, maybe because he saw her eyes, maybe because he had lost interest in the game, or maybe because he had a crush on Frieda, in any case Woodrow looked frightened just long enough to give her more courage.

"Leave her 'lone, or I'm gone tell everybody what you did!"

Woodrow did not answer; he just walled his eyes.

Bay Boy piped up, "Go on, gal. Ain't nobody bothering you."

"You shut up, Bullet Head." I had found my tongue.

"Who you calling Bullet Head?"

"I'm calling you Bullet Head, Bullet Head."

Frieda took Pecola's hand. "Come on."

"You want a fat lip?" Bay Boy drew back his fist at me.

"Yeah. Gimme one of yours."

"You gone get one."

Maureen appeared at my elbow, and the boys seemed reluctant to continue under her springtime eyes so wide with interest. They buckled in confusion, not willing to beat up three girls under her watchful gaze. So they listened to a budding male instinct that told them to pretend we were unworthy of their attention.

"Come on, man."

"Yeah. Come on. We ain't got time to fool with them."

Grumbling a few disinterested epithets, they moved away.

I picked up Pecola's notebook and Frieda's coat, and the four of us left the playground.

"Old Bullet Head, he's always picking on girls."

Frieda agreed with me. "Miss Forrester said he was incorrigival[1]."

"Really?" I didn't know what that meant, but it had enough of a doom sound in it to be true of Bay Boy.

While Frieda and I clucked on about the near fight, Maureen, suddenly animated, put her velvet-sleeved arm through Pecola's and began to behave as though they were the closest of friends.

"I just moved here. My name is Maureen Peal. What's yours?"

"Pecola."

"Pecola? Wasn't that the name of the girl in *Imitation of Life?*"

"I don't know. What is that?"

"The picture show, you know. Where this mulatto girl hates her mother, 'cause she is black and ugly but then cries at the funeral. It was real sad. Everybody cries in it. Claudette Colbert too."

"Oh." Pecola's voice was no more than a sigh.

"Anyway, her name was Pecola too. She was so pretty. When it comes back, I'm going to see it again. My mother has seen it four times."

Frieda and I walked behind them, surprised at Maureen's friendliness to Pecola, but pleased. Maybe she wasn't so bad, after all. Frieda had put her coat back on her head, and the two of us, so draped, trotted along enjoying the warm breeze and Frieda's heroics.

---

[1] *incorrigival:* what Miss Forrester actually said must have been "incorrigible" — so bad that there is no hope of improvement

"You're in my gym class, aren't you?" Maureen asked Pecola.

"Yes."

"Miss Erkmeister's legs sure are bow. I bet she thinks they're cute. How come she gets to wear real shorts, and we have to wear those old bloomers? I want to die every time I put them on."

Pecola smiled but did not look at Maureen.

"Hey." Maureen stopped short. "There's an Isaley's. Want some ice cream? I have money."

She unzipped a hidden pocket in her muff and pulled out a multifolded dollar bill. I forgave her those knee socks.

"My uncle sued Isaley's," Maureen said to the three of us. "He sued the Isaley's in Akron. They said he was disorderly and that that was why they wouldn't serve him, but a friend of his, a policeman, came in and beared the witness, so the suit went through."

"What's a suit?"

"It's when you can beat them up if you want to and won't anybody do nothing. Our family does it all the time. We believe in suits."

At the entrance to Isaley's, Maureen turned to Frieda and me, asking, "You all going to buy some ice cream?"

We looked at each other. "No," Frieda said.

Maureen disappeared into the store with Pecola.

Frieda looked placidly down the street; I opened my mouth, but quickly closed it. It was extremely important that the world not know that I fully expected Maureen to buy us some ice cream, that for the past one hundred and twenty seconds I had been selecting the flavour, that I had begun to like Maureen, and that neither of us had a penny.

We supposed Maureen was being nice to Pecola because of the boys, and were embarrassed to be caught — even by each other — thinking that she would treat us, or that we deserved it as much as Pecola did.

The girls came out. Pecola with two dips of orange-pineapple, Maureen with black raspberry.

"You should have got some," she said. "They had all kinds. Don't eat down to the tip of the cone," she advised Pecola.

"Why?"

"Because there's a fly in there."

"How you know?"

"Oh, not really. A girl told me she found one in the bottom of hers once, and ever since then she throws that part away."

"Oh."

We passed the Dreamland Theatre, and Betty Grable smiled down at us.

"Don't you just love her?" Maureen asked.

"Uh-huh," said Pecola.

I differed. "Hedy Lamarr is better."

Maureen agreed. "Ooooo yes. My mother told me that a girl named Audrey, she went to the beauty parlour where we lived before, and asked the lady to fix her hair like Hedy Lamarr's, and the lady said, 'Yeah, when you grow some hair like Hedy Lamarr's.'" She laughed long and sweet.

"Sounds crazy," said Frieda.

"She sure is. Do you know she doesn't even menstruate yet, and she's sixteen. Do you, yet?"

"Yes." Pecola glanced at us.

"So do I." Maureen made no attempt to disguise her pride. "Two months ago I started. My girl friend in Toledo, where we lived before, said when she started she was scared to death. Thought she had killed herself."

"Do you know what it's for?" Pecola asked the question as though hoping to provide the answer herself.

"For babies." Maureen raised two pencil-stroke eyebrows at the obviousness of the question. "Babies need blood when they are inside you, and if you are having a baby, then you don't menstruate. But when you're not having a baby, then you don't have to save the blood, so it comes out."

"How do babies get the blood?" asked Pecola.

"Through the like-line. You know. Where your belly button is. That is where the like-line grows from and pumps the blood to the baby."

"Well, if the belly buttons are to grow like-lines to give the baby blood, and only girls have babies, how come boys have belly buttons?"

Maureen hesitated. "I don't know," she admitted. "But boys have all sorts of things they don't need." Her tinkling laughter was somehow stronger than our nervous ones. She curled her tongue around the edge of the cone, scooping up a dollop of purple that made my eyes water. We were waiting for a stop light to change. Maureen kept scooping the ice cream from around the cone's edge with her tongue; she didn't bite the edge as I would have done. Her tongue circled the cone. Pecola had finished hers; Maureen evidently liked her things to last. While I was thinking about her ice cream, she must have been thinking about her last remark, for she said to Pecola, "Did you ever see a naked man?"

Pecola blinked, then looked away. "No. Where would I see a naked man?"

"I don't know. I just asked."

"I wouldn't even look at him, even if I did see him. That's dirty. Who wants to see a naked man?" Pecola was agitated. "Nobody's father would be naked in front of his own daughter. Not unless he was dirty too."

"I didn't say 'father'. I just said 'a naked man'."

"Well ..."

"How come you said 'father'?" Maureen wanted to know.

"Who else would she see, dog tooth?" I was glad to have a chance to show anger. Not only because of the ice cream, but because we had seen our own father naked and didn't care to be reminded of it and feel the shame brought on by the absence of shame. He had been walking down the hall from the bathroom into his bedroom and passed the open door of our room. We had lain there wide-eyed. He stopped and looked in, trying to see in the dark room whether we were really asleep — or was it his imagination that opened eyes were looking at him? Apparently he convinced himself that we were sleeping. He moved away, confident that his little girls would not lie open-eyed like that, staring, staring. When he had moved on, the dark took only him away, not his nakedness. That stayed in the room with us. Friendly-like.

"I'm not talking to you," said Maureen. "Besides, I don't care if she sees her father naked. She can look at him all day if she wants to. Who cares?"

"You do," said Frieda. "That's all you talk about."

"It is not."

"It is so. Boys, babies, and somebody's naked daddy. You must be boy crazy."

"You better be quiet."

"Who's gonna make me?" Frieda put her hand on her hip and jutted her face toward Maureen.

"You all ready made. Mammy made."

"You stop talking about my mama."

"Well, you stop talking about my daddy."

"Who said anything about your old daddy?"

"You did."

"Well, you started it."

"I wasn't even talking to you. I was talking to Pecola."

"Yeah. About seeing her naked daddy."

"So what if she did see him?"

Pecola shouted, "I never saw my daddy naked. Never."

"You did too," Maureen snapped. "Bay Boy said so."

"I did not."

"You did."

"I did not."

"Did. Your own daddy, too!"

Pecola tucked her head in — a funny, sad, helpless movement. A kind of hunching of the shoulders, pulling in of the neck, as though she wanted to cover her ears.

"You stop talking about her daddy," I said.

"What do I care about her old black daddy?" asked Maureen.

"Black? Who you calling black?"

"You!"

"You think you so cute!" I swung at her and missed, hitting Pecola in the face. Furious at my clumsiness, I threw my notebook at her, but it caught her in the small of her velvet back, for she had turned and was flying across the street against traffic.

Safe on the other side, she screamed at us, "I *am* cute! And you ugly! Black and ugly black e mos. I *am* cute!"

She ran down the street, the green knee socks making her legs look like wild dandelion stems that had somehow lost their heads. The weight of her remark stunned us, and it was a second or two before Frieda and I collected ourselves enough to shout, "Six-finger-dog-tooth-meringue-pie!" We chanted this most powerful of our arsenal of insults as long as we could see the green stems and rabbit fur.

Grown people frowned at the three girls on the kerbside, two with their coats draped over their heads, the collars framing the eyebrows like nuns' habits, black garters showing where they bit the tops of brown stockings that barely covered the knees, angry faces knotted like dark cauliflowers.

Pecola stood a little apart from us, her eyes hinged in the direction in which Maureen had fled. She seemed to fold into herself, like a pleated wing. Her pain antagonised me. I wanted to open her up, crisp her edges, ram a stick down that hunched and curving spine, force her to stand erect and spit the misery out on the streets. But she held it in where it could lap up into her eyes.

Frieda snatched her coat from her head. "Come on, Claudia. 'Bye, Pecola."

We walked quickly at first, and then slower, pausing every now and then to fasten garters, tie shoelaces, scratch, or examine old scars. We were sinking under the wisdom, accuracy, and relevance of Maureen's last words. If she was cute — and if anything could be believed, she *was* — then we were not. And what did that mean? We were lesser. Nicer, brighter, but still lesser. Dolls we could destroy, but we could not destroy the honey voices of parents and aunts, the obedience in the eyes of our peers, the slippery light in the eyes of our teachers when they encountered the Maureen Peals of the world. What was the secret? What did we lack? Why was it important? And so what? Guileless and without vanity, we were still in love with ourselves then. We felt comfortable in our skins, enjoyed the news that our senses released to us, admired our dirt, cultivated our scars, and could not comprehend this unworthiness. Jealousy we understood and thought natural — a desire to have what somebody else had; but envy was a strange, new feeling for us. And all the time we knew that Maureen Peal was not the Enemy and not worthy of such intense hatred. The *Thing* to fear was the *Thing* that made *her* beautiful, and not us.

The Distant One

by Michael Anthony

Trinidad, in the West Indies: the oldest son, Albert, left some time ago for England, and we see the parting through the eyes of his younger brother, Leroy.

The Distant One

It didn't seem such a long time that Albert was away. At least not a year. How the months had flown! A year since Albert was packing, since...

The boy sat up on the bed with the scene vivid in his mind. He relived all the excitement, and pain, and the emptiness of the days that followed: they all came back to his mind this morning. Really, they had never left him. But this morning the pain cut deeper, and the emptiness was more complete.

The other members of the household, though, were up and stirring. The other children had already changed from their night clothes, and were getting busy as usual. The mother hurried about the house, sweeping, dusting, and dashing into and out of the kitchen. Once or twice she glanced from the corner of her eyes at the little boy sitting there on the bed. Now she glanced again and he was still there. "I wonder what's Leroy's intention this morning!" she said aloud, half of herself, and half sharply; but she went about her chores.

Leroy had indeed been day-dreaming. If any sound came to him it must have come from far away. For his own spinning top was in his mind's eye.

He was recalling the very morning that top was made. He could see Albert now, bending over the laguette wood, chopping, chopping, until gradually — almost magically — a brand new top was born. Then Albert had taken a nail from his pocket, moved over the fireplace to heat it, and as easily as ever he had made the hot nail go into the wood. He had got the exact depth, then he put the top in water to cool the nail off. Then he had said, "Here, Lee, try it out!" And Albert had watched Lee put on the marling twine, and when he had released the top from the twine with a zing, they were both amazed to see how perfectly it spun, and for him it was the best top in the world. "It's yours, Lee!" Albert had said then. Leroy had been so surprised and glad that words failed to come. From that moment it had come home to him that he and Albert were real, real pals, closer than anything.

All these thoughts were flooding back to him now and he was completely carried away.

"Leroy!"

The mother's voice was sharp, almost thunderous, so that the boy, completely startled, felt his heart jump. But the next moment he had regained his senses and was now hustling out of his pyjamas and hurrying into home clothes.

The mother did not have to say any more because Leroy's task was clear cut.

He was out into the yard now. He hurried to the goats — for he should have already been on his way to the tethering place — and though the top was in his pocket, this morning there would be no time for a *one-line* game.

The morning sun had already struck the pitch road. He felt the surface warm and pleasant to his feet. The goats must have felt the same, for instead of walking on the roadside grass, they walked in the centre of the road. Albert had never pulled them away when they walked in the centre of the road. Only when a car came hurtling up. And in the evening when he went for them again he did not have to lead them for they knew the house and were anxious. And they trusted Albert. When he stood up they stood up, too, and when he started again they started. And now the goats were here and Albert was not here, and the sun made it warm underfoot. That was funny. The boy smiled wistfully to himself, and he could not help wondering whether the sun made it warm under Albert's feet, too, this morning, wherever he was in that England place.

It was different when the last letter had come. Albert had said it was not too bad but it was cold. He had mentioned that there was so much to see and so many places to go to, and it would have been very nice had it not been cold. And then he wrote to ask about Leroy. With this thought the boy felt a sharp pain, which, though he was not tired, made his breath come in gasps. He remembered the letter vividly for he had taken it to school with him and must have read it a hundred times. He and his friends. He had been so proud, but now it was already a long time.

He must write to Albert. He had tried several times but whenever he took up the pen he could not find words to say. But he must write. For Meggy had kids again, and one had died. And the mango trees in Spring Flat were yellow with fruit. And the top — he hung his head, for he would not tell about the nail-hole — the top was still good and he wouldn't play *one-line* with it!

Were it not for the goats he might have walked on past the savannah. But the goats turned off the road, almost dragging him with them. "Scamps!" he said, as if he realised they had a point on him. And he looked for where the grass was greenest and began driving in his stakes.

The mother tried to be her usual self in spite of everything. She was always up and doing, busy as ever about the house. She made it a point of duty to be so. For she realised that not only did she have to take Albert off the children's mind but off her own mind as well. She could not have carried on if she had allowed the terrible longing to take possession of her. The boy had gone away for a few years only. He had been determined to go and he had worked and had saved his own money. She hoped he made good there because she had counted on his coming back and helping her with the smaller ones. And naturally she was longing to see him again. In the first place, it was not easy letting him go.

She always thought of him but she had fought hard to suppress her feelings. Especially in the light of the children, and particularly so in the light of Leroy, who, if given a moment to himself, would fall into brooding and dream.

She roused herself from her thoughts. Was she not dreaming, too? She busied herself sweeping out the house and then she went outside to wash some clothes. Then she went in and took up the shopbag as she heard the drone of the mail-bus. She would go to the shop first, then in coming back she would look in at the Post Office. She would not have to go in for she was sure the lady in the Post Office would look out and signal "No". Or maybe ... who knows?

As it turned out the lady in the Post Office looked out and signalled "No". The mother turned back with pain and took the road up the hill. Seeing that she was broken-spirited the lady in the Post Office called out, "Perhaps tomorrow, Mrs Austin".

Mrs Austin turned back and forced a smile. "Perhaps. I'll send the little boy."

There were no letters that week. Nor the next week, nor the next. But some time in the following week the postmistress looked out for when the boy was passing and hailed to him and signalled to him to come.

The boy ran up the road gingerly, and received the letter, and both he and the postmistress laughed. Then he sped up the hill to his home.

The family huddled together to read the letter. The children, including Leroy, read with difficulty, because the words were long and they had not learnt them yet. But it was not long before the mother finished and she went back to the kitchen. Then she went back out to the children and she said, "I don't think he said exactly when he'll come but it won't be long now. Let me see ..." She took the letter away and went into the kitchen. And she said to herself: "Oh, is so? England nice. Trinidad too backward. He playing man already. Okay, let him stay there. We'll live without him." And she called out, "Leroy, go and give the goats water!"

I Spy

by Graham Greene

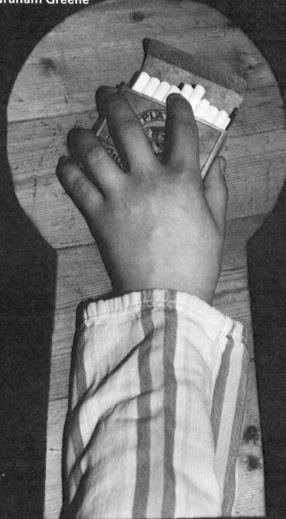

It is during the Second World War; Charlie's father keeps a small tobacconist's shop. Why was he away that night? Charlie doesn't know, and so we don't know. But as Charlie has forced himself to steal some cigarettes in the middle of the night he sees his father in a new light.

I Spy

Charlie Stowe waited until he heard his mother snore before he got out of bed. Even then he moved with caution and tiptoed to the window. The front of the house was irregular, so that it was possible to see a light burning in his mother's room. But now all the windows were dark. A searchlight passed across the sky, lighting the banks of cloud and probing the dark deep spaces between, seeking enemy airships. The wind blew from the sea, and Charlie Stowe could hear behind his mother's snores the beating of the waves. A draught through the cracks in the window-frame stirred his nightshirt. Charlie Stowe was frightened.

But the thought of the tobacconist's shop which his father kept down a dozen wooden stairs drew him on. He was twelve years old, and already boys at the County School mocked him because he had never smoked a cigarette. The packets were piled twelve deep below, Gold Flake and Players, De Reszke, Abdulla, Woodbines, and the little shop lay under a thin haze of stale smoke which would completely disguise his crime. That it was a crime to steal some of his father's stock Charlie Stowe had no doubt, but he did not love his father; his father was unreal to him, a wraith, pale, thin, indefinite, who noticed him only spasmodically and left even punishment to his mother. For his mother he felt a passionate demonstrative love; her large boisterous presence and her noisy charity filled the world for him; from her speech he judged her the friend of everyone, from the rector's wife to the "dear Queen", except the "Huns", the monsters who lurked in Zeppelins in the clouds. But his father's affection and dislike were as indefinite as his movements. Tonight he had said he would be in Norwich, and yet you never knew. Charlie Stowe had no sense of safety as he crept down the wooden stairs. When they creaked he clenched his fingers on the collar of his nightshirt.

At the bottom of the stairs he came out quite suddenly into the little shop. It was too dark to see his way, and he did not dare touch the switch. For half a minute he sat in despair on the bottom step with his chin cupped in his hands. Then the regular movement of the searchlight was reflected through an upper window and the boy had time to fix in memory the pile of cigarettes, the counter, and the small hole under it. The footsteps of a policeman on the pavement made him grab the first packet to his hand and dive for the hole. A light shone along the floor and a hand tried the door, then the footsteps passed on, and Charlie cowered in the darkness.

At last he got his courage back by telling himself in his curiously adult way that if he were caught now there was nothing to be done about it, and he might as well have his smoke. He put a cigarette in his mouth and then remembered that he had no matches. For awhile he dared not move. Three times the searchlight lit the shop, as he muttered taunts and encouragements. "May as well be hung for a sheep," "Cowardy, cowardy custard," grown-up and childish exhortations oddly mixed.

But as he moved he heard footfalls in the street, the sound of several men walking rapidly. Charlie Stowe was old enough to feel surprise that anybody was about. The footsteps came nearer, stopped; a key was turned in the shop door, a voice said: "Let him in," and then he heard his father, "If you wouldn't mind being quiet, gentlemen. I don't want to wake up the family." There was a note unfamiliar to Charlie in the undecided voice. A torch flashed and the electric globe burst into blue light. The boy held his breath; he wondered whether his father would hear his heart beating, and he clutched his nightshirt tightly and prayed, "O God, don't let me be caught." Through a crack in the counter he could see his father where he stood, one hand held to his high stiff collar, between two men in bowler hats and belted mackintoshes. They were strangers.

"Have a cigarette," his father said in a voice dry as a biscuit. One of the men shook his head. "It wouldn't do, not when we are on duty. Thank you all the same." He spoke gently, but without kindness: Charlie Stowe thought his father must be ill.

"Mind if I put a few in my pocket?" Mr Stowe asked, and when the man nodded he lifted a pile of Gold Flake and Players from a shelf and caressed the packets with the tips of his fingers.

"Well," he said, "there's nothing to be done about it, and I may as well have my smokes." For a moment Charlie Stowe feared discovery, his father stared round the shop so thoroughly; he might have been seeing it for the first time. "It's a good little business," he said, "for those that like it. The wife will sell out, I suppose. Else the neighbours'll be wrecking it. Well, you want to be off. A stitch in time. I'll get my coat."

"One of us'll come with you, if you don't mind," said the stranger gently.

"You needn't trouble. It's on the peg here. There, I'm all ready."

The other man said in an embarrassed way, "Don't you want to speak to your wife?" The thin voice was decided. "Not me. Never do today what you can put off till tomorrow. She'll have her chance later, won't she?"

"Yes, yes," one of the strangers said and he became very cheerful and encouraging. "Don't you worry too much. While there's life..." and suddenly his father tried to laugh.

When the door had closed Charlie Stowe tiptoed upstairs and got into bed. He wondered why his father had left the house again so late at night and who the strangers were. Surprise and awe kept him for a little while awake. It was as if a familiar photograph had stepped from the frame to reproach him with neglect. He remembered how his father had held tight to his collar and fortified himself with proverbs, and he thought for the first time that, while his mother was boisterous and kindly, his father was very like himself, doing things in the dark which frightened him. It would have pleased him to go down to his father and tell him that he loved him, but he could hear through the window the quick steps going away. He was alone in the house with his mother, and he fell asleep.

Where Are You Going, Where Have You Been?

by Joyce Carol Oates

Connie lives in a single-storey house (a "ranch house") three miles from the nearest town in a country part of the United States of America. She is fifteen, and reckons herself rather sophisticated. One Sunday when she refuses to go with her parents to relatives, she is left alone. Two men drive up. They do not use violence, but they exert a force on her that is difficult to resist.

Where Are You Going, Where Have You Been?

Her name was Connie. She was fifteen and she had a quick, nervous giggling habit of craning her neck to glance into mirrors or checking other people's faces to make sure her own was all right. Her mother, who noticed everything and knew everything and who hadn't much reason any longer to look at her own face, always scolded Connie about it. "Stop gawking at yourself. Who are you? You think you're so pretty?" she would say. Connie would raise her eyebrows at these familiar old complaints and look right through her mother, into a shadowy vision of herself as she was right at that moment: she knew she was pretty and that was everything. Her mother had been pretty once too, if you could believe those old snapshots in the album, but now her looks were gone and that was why she was always after Connie.

"Why don't you keep your room clean like your sister? How've you got your hair fixed — what the hell stinks? Hair spray? You don't see your sister using that junk."

Her sister June was twenty-four and still lived at home. She was a secretary in the high school Connie attended, and if that wasn't bad enough—with her in the same building—she was so plain and chunky and steady that Connie had to hear her praised all the time by her mother and her mother's sisters. June did this, June did that, she saved money and helped clean the house and cooked and Connie couldn't do a thing, her mind was all filled with trashy daydreams. Their father was away at work most of the time and when he came home he wanted supper and he read the newspaper at supper and after supper he went to bed. He didn't bother talking much to them, but around his bent head Connie's mother kept picking at her until Connie wished her mother was dead and she herself was dead and it was all over. "She makes me want to throw up sometimes," she complained to her friends. She had a high, breathless, amused voice that made everything she said sound a little forced, whether it was sincere or not.

There was one good thing: June went places with girl friends of hers, girls who were just as plain and steady as she, and so when Connie wanted to do that her mother had no objections. The father of Connie's best girl friend drove the girls the three miles to town and left them at a shopping plaza so they could walk through the stores or go to a movie, and when he came to pick them up again at eleven he never bothered to ask what they had done.

They must have been familiar sights, walking around the shopping plaza in their shorts and flat ballerina slippers that always scuffed on the sidewalk, with charm bracelets jingling on their thin wrists; they would lean together to whisper and laugh secretly if someone passed who amused or interested them. Connie had long dark blond hair that drew anyone's eye to it, and she wore part of it pulled up on her head and puffed out and the rest of it she let fall down her back. She wore a pull-over jersey blouse that looked one way when she was at home and another way when she was away from home. Everything about her had two sides to it, one for home and one for anywhere that was not home: her walk, which could be childlike and bobbing, or languid enough to make anyone think she was hearing music in her head; her mouth, which was pale and smirking most of the time, but bright and pink on these evenings out; her laugh, which was cynical and drawling at home—"Ha, ha, very funny,"—but highpitched and nervous anywhere else, like the jingling of the charms on her bracelet.

Sometimes they did go shopping or to a movie, but sometimes they went across the highway, ducking fast across the busy road, to a drive-in restaurant where older kids hung out. The restaurant was shaped like a big bottle though squatter than a real bottle, and on its cap was a revolving figure of a grinning boy holding a hamburger aloft. One night in midsummer they ran across, breathless with daring, and right away someone leaned out a car window and invited them over, but it was just a boy from high school they didn't like. It made them feel good to be able to ignore him. They went up through the maze of parked and cruising cars to the bright-lit, fly-infested restaurant, their faces pleased and expectant as if they were entering a sacred building that loomed up out of the night to give them what haven and blessing they yearned for. They sat at the counter and crossed their legs at the ankles, their thin shoulders rigid with excitement, and listened to the music that made everything so good: the music was always in the background, like music at a church service; it was something to depend upon.

A boy named Eddie came in to talk with them. He sat backwards on his stool, turning himself jerkily around in semicircles and then stopping and turning back again, and after a while he asked Connie if she would like something to eat. She said she would so she tapped her friend's arm on her way out — her friend pulled her face up into a brave, droll look—and Connie said she would meet her at eleven across the way. "I just hate to leave her like that," Connie said earnestly, but the boy said that she wouldn't be alone for long. So they went out to his car, and on the way Connie couldn't help but let her eyes wander over the windshields and faces all around her, her face gleaming with a joy that had nothing to do with Eddie or even this place; it might have been the music. She drew her shoulders up and sucked in her breath with the pure pleasure of being alive, and just at that moment she happened to glance at a face just a few feet away from hers. It was a boy with shaggy black hair, in a convertible jalopy painted gold. He stared at her and then his lips widened into a grin. Connie slit her eyes at him and turned away, but she couldn't help glancing back and there he was, still watching her. He wagged a finger and laughed and said, "Gonna get you, baby," and Connie turned away again without Eddie noticing anything.

She spent three hours with him, at the restaurant where they ate hamburgers and drank Cokes in wax cups that were always sweating, and then down an alley a mile or so away, and when he left her off at five to eleven only the movie house was still open at the plaza. Her girl friend was there, talking with a boy. When Connie came up, the two girls smiled at each other and Connie said, "How was the movie?" and the girl said, "*You* should know." They rode off with the girl's father, sleepy and pleased, and Connie couldn't help but look back at the darkened shopping plaza with its big empty parking lot and its signs that were faded and ghostly now, and over at the drive-in restaurant where cars were still circling tirelessly. She couldn't hear the music at this distance.

Next morning June asked her how the movie was and Connie said, "So-so."

She and that girl and occasionally another girl went out several times a week, and the rest of the time Connie spent around the house—it was summer vacation—getting in her mother's way and thinking, dreaming about the boys she met. But all the boys fell back and dissolved into a single face that was not even a face but an idea, a feeling, mixed up with the urgent insistent pounding of the music and the humid night air of July. Connie's mother kept dragging her back to the daylight by finding things for her to do or saying suddenly, "What's this about the Pettinger girl?"

And Connie would say nervously, "Oh, her. That dope." She always drew thick clear lines between herself and such girls, and her mother was simple and kind enough to believe it. Her mother was so simple, Connie thought, that it was maybe cruel to fool her so much. Her mother went scuffling around the house in old bedroom slippers and complained over the telephone to one sister about the other, then the other called up and the two of them complained about the third one. If June's name was mentioned her mother's tone was approving, and if Connie's name was mentioned it was disapproving. This did not really mean she disliked Connie, and actually Connie thought that her mother preferred her to June just because she was prettier, but the two of them kept up a pretense of exasperation, a sense that they were tugging and struggling over something of little value to either of them. Sometimes, over coffee, they were almost friends, but something would come up—some vexation that was like a fly buzzing suddenly around their heads—and their faces went hard with contempt.

One Sunday Connie got up at eleven — none of them bothered with church — and washed her hair so that it could dry all day long in the sun. Her parents and sister were going to a barbecue at an aunt's house and Connie said no, she wasn't interested, rolling her eyes to let her mother know just what she thought of it. "Stay home alone then," her mother said sharply. Connie sat out back in a lawn chair and watched them drive away, her father quiet and bald, hunched around so that he could back the car out, her mother with a look that was still angry and not at all softened through the windshield and in the back seat poor old June, all dressed up as if she didn't know what a barbecue was, with all the running yelling kids and the flies. Connie sat with her eyes closed in the sun, dreaming and dazed with the warmth about her as if this were a kind of love, the caresses of love, and her mind slipped over onto thoughts of the boy she had been with the night before and how nice he had been, how sweet it always was, not the way someone like June would suppose but sweet, gentle, the way it was in movies and promised in songs; and when she opened her eyes she hardly knew where she was, the back yard ran off into weeds and a fence-like line of trees and behind it the sky was perfectly blue and still. The asbestos "ranch house" that was now three years old startled her — it looked small. She shook her head as if to get awake.

It was too hot. She went inside the house and turned on the radio to drown out the quiet. She sat on the edge of her bed, barefoot, listened for an hour and a half, to a programme called XYZ Sunday Jamboree, record after record of hard, fast, shrieking songs she sang along with, interspersed by exclamations from "Bobby King": "An' look here, you girls at Napoleon's — Son and Charley want you to pay real close attention to this song coming up!"

And Connie paid close attention herself, bathed in a glow of slow-pulsed joy that seemed to rise mysteriously out of the music itself and lay languidly about the airless little room, breathed in and breathed out with each gentle rise and fall of her chest.

After a while she heard a car coming up the drive. She sat up at once, startled, because it couldn't be her father so soon. The gravel kept crunching all the way in from the road — the driveway was long — and Connie ran to the window. It was a car she didn't know. It was an open jalopy, painted a bright gold that caught the sunlight opaquely. Her heart began to pound and her fingers snatched at her hair, checking it, and she whispered, "Christ, Christ," wondering how she looked. The car came to a stop at the side door and the horn sounded four short taps, as if this were a signal Connie knew.

She went into the kitchen and approached the door slowly, then hung out the screen door, her bare toes curling down off the step. There were two boys in the car and now she recognised the driver: he had shaggy, shabby black hair that looked crazy as a wig and he was grinning at her.

"I ain't late, am I?" he said.

"Who the hell do you think you are?" Connie said.

"Toldja I'd be out, didn't I?"

"I don't even know who you are."

She spoke sullenly, careful to show no interest or pleasure, and he spoke in a fast, bright monotone. Connie looked past him to the other boy, taking her time. He had fair brown hair, with a lock that fell onto his forehead. His sideburns gave him a fierce, embarrassed look, but so far he hadn't even bothered to glance at her. Both boys wore sunglasses. The driver's glasses were metallic and mirrored everything in miniature.

"You wanta come for a ride?" he said.

Connie smirked and let her hair fall loose over one shoulder.

"Don'tcha like my car? New paint job," he said. "Hey."

"What?"

"You're cute."

She pretended to fidget, chasing flies away from the door.

"Don'tcha believe me, or what?" he said.

"Look, I don't even know who you are," Connie said in disgust.

"Hey, Ellie's got a radio, see. Mine broke down." He lifted his friend's arm and showed her the little transistor radio the boy was holding, and now Connie began to hear the music. It was the same programme that was playing inside the house.

"Bobby King?" she said.

"I listen to him all the time. I think he's great."

"He's kind of great," Connie said reluctantly.

"Listen, that guy's *great*. He knows where the action is."

Connie blushed a little, because the glasses made it impossible for her to see just what this boy was looking at. She couldn't decide if she liked him or if he was a jerk, and so she dawdled in the doorway and wouldn't come down or go back inside. She said, "What's all that stuff painted on your car?"

"Can'tcha read it?" He opened the door very carefully, as if he were afraid it might fall off. He slid out just as carefully, planting his feet firmly on the ground, the tiny metallic world in his glasses slowing down like gelatine hardening, and in the midst of it Connie's bright green blouse. "This here is my name, to begin with," he said. ARNOLD FRIEND was written in tarlike black letters on the side, with a drawing of a round, grinning face that reminded Connie of a pumpkin, except it wore sunglasses. "I wanta introduce myself. I'm Arnold Friend and that's my real name and I'm gonna be your friend, honey, and inside the car's Ellie Oscar, he's kinda shy." Ellie brought his transistor radio up to his shoulder and balanced it there. "Now these numbers are a secret code, honey," Arnold Friend explained. He read off the numbers 33, 19, 17 and raised his eyebrows at her to see what she thought of that, but she didn't think much of it. The left rear fender had been smashed and

around it was written, on the gleaming gold background:
DONE BY CRAZY WOMAN DRIVER. Connie had to laugh
at that. Arnold Friend was pleased at her laughter and looked
up at her. "Around the other side's a lot more — you wanta
come and see them?"

"No."

"Why not?"

"Why should I?"

"Don'tcha wanta see what's on the car? Don'tcha wanta go
for a ride?"

"I don't know."

"Why not?"

"I got things to do."

"Like what?"

"Things."

He laughed as if she had said something funny. He slapped
his thighs. He was standing in a strange way, leaning back
against the car as if he were balancing himself. He wasn't tall,
only an inch or so taller than she would be if she came down to
him. Connie liked the way he was dressed, which was the way
all of them dressed: tight faded jeans stuffed into black, scuffed
boots, a belt that pulled his waist in and showed how lean he
was, and a white pull-over shirt that was a little soiled and
showed the hard small muscles of his arms and shoulders. He
looked as if he probably did hard work, lifting and carrying
things. Even his neck looked muscular. And his face was a
familiar face, somehow; the jaw and chin and cheeks slightly
darkened because he hadn't shaved for a day or two, and the
nose long and hawklike, sniffing as if she were a treat he was
going to gobble up and it was all a joke.

"Connie, you ain't telling the truth. This is your day set aside
for a ride with me and you know it," he said, still laughing. The
way he straightened and recovered from his fit of laughing
showed that it had been all fake.

"How do you know what my name is?" she said suspiciously.

"It's Connie."

"Maybe and maybe not."

"I know my Connie," he said, wagging his finger. Now she
remembered him even better, back at the restaurant, and her
cheeks warmed at the thought of how she had sucked in her
breath just at the moment she passed him — how she must have
looked to him. And he had remembered her. "Ellie and I come

out here especially for you," he said. "Ellie can sit in back. How about it?"

"Where?"

"Where're we going?"

He looked at her. He took off the sunglasses and she saw how pale the skin around his eyes was, like holes that were not in shadow but instead in light. His eyes were like chips of broken glass that catch the light in an amiable way. He smiled. It was as if the idea of going for a ride somewhere, to someplace, was a new idea to him.

"Just for a ride, Connie sweetheart."

"I never said my name was Connie," she said.

"But I know what it is. I know your name and all about you, lots of things," Arnold Friend said. He had not moved yet but stood still leaning back against the side of his jalopy. "I took a special interest in you, such a pretty girl, and found out all about you — like I know your parents and sister are gone somewheres and I know where and how long they're going to be gone, and I know who you were with last night, and your best girl friend's name is Betty. Right?"

He spoke in a simple lilting voice, exactly as if he were reciting the words to a song. His smile assured her that everything was fine. In the car Ellie turned up the volume on his radio and did not bother to look around at them.

"Ellie can sit in the back seat," Arnold Friend said. He indicated his friend with a casual jerk of his chin, as if Ellie did not count and she should not bother with him.

"How'd you find out all that stuff?" Connie said.

"Listen: Betty Schultz and Tony Fitch and Jimmy Pettinger and Nancy Pettinger," he said in a chant. "Raymond Stanley and Bob Hutter —"

"Do you know all those kids?"

"I know everybody."

"Look, you're kidding. You're not from around here."

"Sure."

"But — how come we never saw you before?"

"Sure you saw me before," he said. He looked down at his boots, as if he were a little offended. "You just don't remember."

"I guess I'd remember you," Connie said.

"Yeah?" He looked up at this, beaming. He was pleased. He began to mark time with the music from Ellie's radio, tapping his fists lightly together. Connie looked away from his smile to the car, which was painted so bright it almost hurt her eyes to look at it. She looked at that name ARNOLD FRIEND. And up at the front fender was an expression that was familiar — MAN THE FLYING SAUCERS. It was an expression kids had used the year before but didn't use this year. She looked at it for a while as if the words meant something to her that she did not yet know.

"What're you thinking about? Huh?" Arnold Friend demanded. "Not worried about your hair blowing around in the car, are you?"

"No."

"Think I maybe can't drive good?"

"How do I know?"

"You're a hard girl to handle. How come?" he said. "Don't you know I'm your friend? Didn't you see me put my sign in the air when you walked by?"

"What sign?"

"My sign." And he drew and X in the air, leaning out toward her. They were maybe ten feet apart. After his hand fell back to his side the X was still in the air, almost visible. Connie let the screen door close and stood perfectly still inside it, listening to the music from her radio and the boy's blend together. She stared at Arnold Friend. He stood there so stiffly relaxed, pretending to be relaxed, with one hand idly on the door handle as if he were keeping himself up that way and had no intention of ever moving again. She recognised most things about him, the tight jeans that showed his thighs and buttocks and the greasy leather boots and the tight shirt, and even that slippery friendly smile of his, that sleepy dreamy smile that all the boys used to get across ideas they didn't want to put into words. She recognised all this and also the sing-song way he talked, slightly mocking, kidding, but serious and a little melancholy, and she recognised the way he tapped one fist against the other in homage to the perpetual music behind him. But all these things did not come together.

She said suddenly, "Hey, how old are you?"

His smile faded. She could see then that he wasn't a kid, he was much older — thirty, maybe more. At this knowledge her heart began to pound faster.

"That's a crazy thing to ask. Can'tcha see I'm your own age?"

"Like hell you are."

"Or maybe a coupla years older. I'm eighteen."

"Eighteen?" she said doubtfully.

He grinned to reassure her and lines appeared at the corners of his mouth. His teeth were big and white. He grinned so broadly his eyes became slits and she saw how thick the lashes were, thick and black as if painted with a black tarlike material. Then, abruptly, he seemed to become embarrassed and looked over his shoulder at Ellie. "*Him*, he's crazy," he said. "Ain't he a riot? He's a nut, a real character." Ellie was still listening to the music. His sunglasses told nothing about what he was thinking. He wore a bright orange shirt unbuttoned halfway to show his chest, which was a pale, bluish chest and not muscular like Arnold Friend's. His shirt collar was turned up all around and the very tips of the collar pointed out past his chin as if they were protecting him. He was pressing the transistor radio up against his ear and sat there in a kind of daze, right in the sun.

"He's kinda strange," Connie said.

"Hey, she says you're kinda strange! Kinda strange!" Arnold Friend cried. He pounded on the car to get Ellie's attention. Ellie turned for the first time and Connie saw with shock that he wasn't a kid either — he had a fair, hairless face, cheeks reddened slightly as if the veins grew too close to the surface of his skin, the face of a forty-year-old baby. Connie felt a wave of dizziness rise in her at this sight and she stared at him as if waiting for something to change the shock of the moment, make it all right again. Ellie's lips kept shaping words, mumbling along with the words blasting in his ear.

"Maybe you two better go away," Connie said faintly.

"What? How come?" Arnold Friend cried. "We come out here to take you for a ride. It's Sunday." He had the voice of the man on the radio now. It was the same voice, Connie thought. "Don'tcha know it's Sunday all day? And honey, no matter who you were with last night, today you're with Arnold Friend and don't you forget it! Maybe you better step out here," he said, and this last was in a different voice. It was a little flatter, as if the heat was finally getting to him.

"No. I got things to do."

"Hey."

"You two better leave."

"We ain't leaving until you come with us."

"Like hell I am —"

"Connie, don't fool around with me. I mean — I mean, don't

fool *around*," he said, shaking his head. He laughed incredulously. He placed his sunglasses on top of his head, carefully, as if he were indeed wearing a wig, and brought the stems down behind his ears. Connie stared at him, another wave of dizziness and fear rising in her so that for a moment he wasn't even in focus but was just a blur standing there against his gold car, and she had the idea that he had driven up the driveway all right but had come from nowhere before that and belonged nowhere and that everything about him and even about the music that was so familiar to her was only half real.

"If my father comes and sees you —"

"He ain't coming. He's at a barbecue."

"How do you know that?"

"Aunt Tillie's. Right now they're — uh — they're drinking. Sitting around," he said vaguely, squinting as if he were staring all the way to town and over to Aunt Tillie's back yard. Then the vision seemed to get clear and he nodded energetically. "Yeah. Sitting around. There's your sister in a blue dress, huh? And high heels, the poor sad bitch — nothing like you, sweetheart! And your mother's helping some fat woman with the corn, they're cleaning the corn — husking the corn —"

"What fat woman?" Connie cried.

"How do I know what fat woman, I don't know every goddamn fat woman in the world!" Arnold Friend laughed.

"Oh, that's Mrs Hornsby... Who invited her?" Connie said. She felt a little light-headed. Her breath was coming quickly.

"She's too fat. I don't like them fat. I like them the way you are, honey," he said, smiling sleepily at her. They stared at each other for a while through the screen door. He said softly, "Now, what you're going to do is this: you're going to come out that door. You're going to sit up front with me and Ellie's going to sit in the back, the hell with Ellie, right? This isn't Ellie's date. You're my date. I'm your lover, honey."

"What? You're crazy —"

"Yes. I'm your lover. You don't know what that is but you will," he said. "I know that too. I know all about you. But look: it's real nice and you couldn't ask for nobody better than me, or more polite. I always keep my word. I'll tell you how it is, I'm always nice at first, the first time. I'll hold you so tight you won't think you have to try to get away or pretend anything because you'll know you can't. And I'll come inside you where it's all secret and you'll give in to me and you'll love me —"

"Shut up! You're crazy!" Connie said. She backed away from the door. She put her hands up against her ears as if she'd heard something terrible, something not meant for her. "People don't talk like that, you're crazy," she muttered. Her heart was almost too big now for her chest and its pumping made sweat break out all over her. She looked out to see Arnold Friend pause and then take a step toward the porch, lurching. He almost fell. But, like a clever drunken man, he managed to catch his balance. He wobbled in his high boots and grabbed hold of one of the porch posts.

"Honey?" he said. "You still listening?"

"Get the hell out of here!"

"Be nice, honey. Listen."

"I'm going to call the police −"

He wobbled again and out of the side of his mouth came a fast spat curse, an aside not meant for her to hear. But even this "Christ!" sounded forced. Then he began to smile again. She watched this smile come, awkward as if he were smiling from inside a mask. His whole face was a mask, she thought wildly, tanned down to his throat but then running out as if he had plastered make-up on his face but had forgotten about his throat.

"Honey −? Listen, here's how it is. I always tell the truth and I promise you this: I ain't coming in that house after you."

"You better not! I'm going to call the police if you − if you don't −"

"Honey," he said, talking right through her voice, "honey. I'm not coming in there but you are coming out here. You know why?"

She was panting. The kitchen looked like a place she had never seen before, some room she had run inside but that wasn't good enough, wasn't going to help her. The kitchen window had never had a curtain, after three years, and there were dishes in the sink for her to do − probably − and if you ran your hand across the table you'd probably feel something sticky there.

"You listening, honey? Hey?"

"− going to call the police −"

"Soon as you touch the phone I don't need to keep my promise and can come inside. You won't want that."

She rushed forward and tried to lock the door. Her fingers were shaking. "But why lock it," Arnold Friend said gently, talking right into her face. "It's just a screen door. It's just nothing." One of his boots was at a strange angle, as if his foot wasn't in it. It pointed out to the left, bent at the ankle. "I mean, anybody can break through a screen door and glass and wood and iron or anything else if he needs to, anybody at all, and specially Arnold Friend. If the place got lit up with a fire, honey, you'd come runnin' out into my arms, right into my arms an' safe at home — like you knew I was your lover and'd stopped fooling around. I don't mind a nice shy girl but I don't like no fooling around." Part of those words were spoken with a slight rhythmic lilt, and Connie somehow recognised them — the echo of a song from last year, about a girl rushing into her boy friend's arms and coming home again —

Connie stood barefoot on the linoleum floor, staring at him. "What do you want?" she whispered.

"I want you," he said.

"What?"

"Seen you that night and thought, that's the one, yes sir. I never needed to look anymore."

"But my father's coming back. He's coming to get me. I had to wash my hair first —" She spoke in a dry, rapid voice, hardly raising it for him to hear.

"No, your daddy is not coming and yes, you had to wash your hair and you washed it for me. It's nice and shining and all for me. I thank you sweetheart," he said with a mock bow, but again he almost lost his balance. He had to bend and adjust his boots. Evidently his feet did not go all the way down; the boots must have been stuffed with something so that he would seem taller. Connie stared out at him and behind him at Ellie in the car, who seemed to be looking off toward Connie's right, into nothing. Then Ellie said, pulling the words out of the air one after another as if he were just discovering them, "You want me to pull out the phone?"

"Shut your mouth and keep it shut," Arnold Friend said, his face red from bending over or maybe from embarrassment because Connie had seen his boots. "This ain't none of your business."

"What — what are you doing? What do you want?" Connie said. "If I call the police they'll get you, they'll arrest you —"

"Promise was not to come in unless you touch that phone, and I'll keep that promise," he said. He resumed his erect position and tried to force his shoulders back. He sounded like a hero in a movie, declaring something important. But he spoke too loudly and it was as if he were speaking to someone behind Connie. "I ain't made plans for coming in that house where I don't belong but just for you to come out to me, the way you should. Don't you know who I am?"

"You're crazy," she whispered. She backed away from the door but did not want to go into another part of the house, as if this would give him permission to come through the door. "What do you ... you're crazy, you..."

"Huh? What're you saying, honey?"

Her eyes darted everywhere in the kitchen. She could not remember what it was, this room.

"This is how it is, honey: you come out and we'll drive away, have a nice ride. But if you don't come out we're gonna wait till your people come home and then they're all going to get it."

"You want that telephone pulled out?" Ellie said. He held the radio away from his ear and grimaced, as if without the radio the air was too much for him.

"I toldja shut up, Ellie," Arnold Friend said, "you're deaf, get a hearing aid, right? Fix yourself up. This little girl's no trouble and's gonna be nice to me, so Ellie keep to yourself, this ain't your date — right? Don't hem in on me, don't hog, don't crush, don't bird dog, don't trail me," he said in a rapid, meaningless voice, as if he were running through all the expressions he'd learned but was no longer sure which of them was in style, then rushing on to new ones, making them up with his eyes closed. "Don't crawl under my fence, don't squeeze in my chipmunk hole, don't sniff my glue, suck my popsicle, keep your own greasy fingers on yourself!" He shaded his eyes and peered in at Connie, who was backed against the kitchen table. "Don't mind him, honey, he's just a creep. He's a dope. Right? I'm the boy for you and like I said, you come out here nice like a lady and give me your hand, and nobody else gets hurt, I mean, your nice old bald-headed daddy and your mummy and your sister in her high heels. Because listen: why bring them in this?"

"Leave me alone," Connie whispered.

"Hey, you know that old woman down the road, the one with the chickens and stuff — you know her?"

"She's dead!"

"Dead? What? You know her?" Arnold Friend said.

"She's dead —"

"Don't you like her?"

"She's dead — she's — she isn't here any more —"

"But don't you like her, I mean, you got something against her? Some grudge or something?" Then his voice dipped as if he were conscious of a rudeness. He touched the sunglasses perched up on top of his head as if to make sure they were still there. "Now, you be a good girl."

"What are you going to do?"

"Just two things, or maybe three," Arnold Friend said. "But I promise it won't last long and you'll like me the way you get to like people you're close to. You will. It's all over for you here, so come on out. You don't want your people in any trouble, do you?"

She turned and bumped against a chair or something, hurting her leg, but she ran into the back room and picked up the telephone. Something roared in her ear, a tiny roaring, and she was so sick with fear that she could do nothing but listen to it — the telephone was clammy and very heavy and her fingers groped down to the dial but were too weak to touch it. She began to scream into the phone, into the roaring. She cried out, she cried for her mother, she felt her breath start jerking back and forth in her lungs as if it were something Arnold Friend was stabbing her with again and again with no tenderness. A noisy sorrowful wailing rose all about her and she was locked inside it the way she was locked inside this house.

After a while she could hear again. She was sitting on the floor with her wet back against the wall.

Arnold Friend was saying from the door, "That's a good girl. Put the phone back."

She kicked the phone away from her.

"No, honey. Pick it up. Put it back right."

She picked it up and put it back. The dial tone stopped.

"That's a good girl. Now, you come outside."

She was hollow with what had been fear but what was now just an emptiness. All that screaming had blasted it out of her. She sat, one leg cramped under her, and deep inside her brain was something like a pinpoint of light that kept going and would not let her relax. She thought, I'm not going to see my mother again. She thought, I'm not going to sleep in my bed again. Her bright green blouse was all wet.

Arnold Friend said, in a gentle-loud voice that was like a stage voice, "The place where you came from ain't there any more, and where you had in mind to go is cancelled out. This place you are now — inside your daddy's house — is nothing but a cardboard box I can knock down any time. You know that and always did know it. You hear me?"

She thought, I have got to think. I have got to know what to do.

"We'll go out to a nice field, out in the country here where it smells so nice and it's sunny," Arnold Friend said. "I'll have my arms tight around you so you won't need to try to get away and I'll show you what love is like, what it does. The hell with this house! It looks solid all right," he said. He ran his fingernail down the screen and the noise did not make Connie shiver, as it would have the day before. "Now, put your hand on your heart, honey. Feel that? That feels solid too but we know better. Be nice to me, be sweet like you can because what else is there for a girl like you but to be sweet and pretty and give in? — and get away before her people get back?"

She felt her pounding heart. Her hand seemed to enclose it. She thought for the first time in her life that it was nothing that was hers, that belonged to her, but just a pounding, living thing inside this body that wasn't really hers either.

"You don't want them to get hurt," Arnold Friend went on. "Now, get up, honey. Get up all by yourself."

She stood.

"Now turn this way. That's right. Come over here to me. — Ellie, put that away, didn't I tell you? You dope. You miserable creepy dope," Arnold Friend said. His words were not angry but only part of an incantation. The incantation was kindly. "Now, come out through the kitchen to me, honey, and let's see a smile, try it, you're a brave, sweet little girl and now they're eating corn and hot dogs cooked to bursting over an outdoor fire, and they don't know one thing about you and never did and honey, you're better than them because not a one of them would have done this for you."

Connie felt the linoleum under her feet; it was cool. She brushed her hair back out of her eyes. Arnold Friend let go of the post tentatively and opened his arms for her, his elbows pointing in toward each other and his wrists limp, to show that this was an embarrassed embrace and a little mocking, he didn't want to make her self-conscious.

She put out her hand against the screen. She watched herself push the door slowly open as if she were back safe somewhere in the other doorway, watching this body and this head of long hair moving out into the sunlight where Arnold Friend waited.

"My sweet little blue-eyed girl," he said in a half-sung sigh that had nothing to do with her brown eyes but was taken up just the same by the vast sunlit reaches of the land behind him and on all sides of him — so much land that Connie had never seen before and did not recognise except to know that she was going to it.

Chicken

by Alan Sillitoe

Dave works in a foundry in the Midlands. He has something of a reputation for stealing, but one day the chicken he steals from a roadside makes what for him was an ordinary theft into an extraordinary incident.

Chicken

One Sunday Dave went to visit a workmate from his foundry who lived in the country near Keyworth. On the way back he pulled up by the laneside to light a fag, wanting some warmth under the leaden and freezing sky. A hen strutted from a gap in the hedge, as proud and unconcerned as if it owned the land for miles around. Dave picked it up without even getting off his bike and stuffed it in a sacklike shopping-bag already weighted by a stone of potatoes. He rode off, wobbling slightly, not even time to kill it, preferring in fact the boasting smiles of getting it home alive, in spite of its thumps and noise.

It was nearly tea-time. He left his bike by the back door, and walked through the scullery into the kitchen with his struggling sack held high in sudden light. His mother laughed: "What have you done, picked up somebody's best cat?"

He took off his clips. "It's a live chicken."

"Where the hell did you get that?" She was already suspicious.

"Bought it in Keyworth. A couple of quid. All meat, after you slit its gizzard and peel off the feathers. Make you a nice pillow, mam."

"It's probably got fleas," Bert said.

He took it from the sack, held it by both legs with one hand while he swallowed a cup of tea with the other. It was a fine plump bird, a White Leghorn hen feathered from tail to topnotch. Its eyes were hooded, covered, and it clucked as if about to lay eggs.

"Well," she said, "we'll have it for dinner sometime next week" — and told him to kill it in the backyard so that there'd be no mess in her clean scullery, but really because she couldn't bear to see it slaughtered. Bert and Colin followed him out to see what sort of a job he'd make of it.

He set his cap on the windowsill. "Get me a sharp knife, will you, somebody?"

"Can you manage?" Colin asked.

"Who are you talking to? Listen, I did it every day when I was in Germany — me and the lads, anyway — whenever we went through a farm. I was good at it. I once killed a pig with a sledgehammer. Crept up behind it through all the muck with my boots around my neck, then let smash. It didn't even know what happened. Brained it, first go." He was so lit up by his own story that the chicken flapped out of his grasp, heading for the gate. Bert, knife in hand, dived from the step and gripped it firm: "Here you are, Dave. Get it out of its misery."

Dave forced the neck onto a half-brick, and cut through neatly, ending a crescendo of noise. Blood swelled over the back of his hand, his nose twitching at the smell of it. Then he looked up, grinning at his pair of brothers: "You thought I'd need some help, did you?" He laughed, head back, grizzled wire hair softening in the atmosphere of slowly descending mist: "You can come out now, mam. It's all done." But she stayed wisely by the fire.

Blood seeped between his fingers, making the whole palm sticky, the back of his hand wet and freezing in bitter air. They wanted to get back inside, to the big fruit pie and tea, and the pale blinding fire that gave you spots before the eyes if you gazed at it too long. Dave looked at the twitching rump, his mouth narrow, grey eyes considering, unable to believe it was over so quickly. A feather, minute and beautiful so that he followed it up as far as possible with his eyes, spun and settled on his nose. He didn't fancy knocking it off with the knife-hand. "Bert, flick it away, for Christ's sake!"

The chicken humped under his sticky palm and hopped its way to a corner of the yard. "Catch it," Dave called, "or it'll fly back home. It's tomorrow's dinner."

"I can't," Bert screamed. He'd done so a minute ago, but it was a different matter now, to catch a hen on the rampage with no head.

It tried to batter a way through the wooden door of the lavatory. Dave's well-studded boots slid along the asphalt, and his bones thumped down hard, laying him flat on his back. Full of strength, spirit and decision, it trotted up his chest and onto his face, scattering geranium petals of blood all over his best white shirt. Bert's quick hands descended, but it launched itself from Dave's forehead and off towards the footscraper near the back door. Colin fell on it, unable to avoid its wings spreading sharply into his eyes before doubling away.

Dave swayed on his feet. "Let's get it, quick." But three did not make a circle, and it soared over its own head and the half-brick of its execution, and was off along the pock-marked yard.

You never knew which way it would dive or zigzag. It avoided all hands with uncanny skill, fighting harder now for its life than when it still had a head left to fight for and think with: it was as if the head a few feet away was transmitting accurate messages of warning and direction that it never failed to pick up, an unbreakable line of communication while blood still went through its veins and heart. When it ran over a crust of bread Colin almost expected it to bend its neck and peck at it.

"It'll run down in a bit, like an alarm clock," Dave said, blood over his trousers, coat torn at the elbow, "then we'll get the bleeder." As it ran along the yard the grey December day was stricken by an almost soundless clucking, only half-heard, as if from miles away, yet tangible nevertheless, maybe a diminution of its earlier protests.

The door of the next house but one was open, and when Bert saw the hen go inside he was on his feet and after it. Dave ran too, the sudden thought striking him that maybe it would shoot out of the front door as well and get run over by a trolley bus on Wilford Road. It seemed still to have a brain and mind of its own, determined to elude them after its uncalled-for treatment at their hands. They all entered the house without thinking to knock, hunters in a state of ecstasy at having cornered their prey at last, hardly separated from the tail of the hen.

Kitchen lights were full on, a fire in the contemporary-style grate, with Mr Grady at that moment panning more coal onto it. He was an upright hard-working man who lived out his life in overtime on the building sites, except for the treat of his Sunday tea. His wife was serving food to their three grown kids and a couple of relations. She dropped the plate of salmon and screamed as the headless chicken flew up onto the table, clearly on a last bound of energy, and began to spin crazily over plates and dishes. She stared at the three brothers in the doorway.

"What is it? Oh dear God, what are you doing? What is it?"

Mr Grady stood, a heavy poker in his hand, couldn't speak while the animal reigned over his table, continually hopping and taking off, dropping blood and feathers, its webbed feet scratching silently over butter and trifle, the soundless echo of clucking seeming to come from its gaping and discontinued neck.

Dave, Bert and Colin were unable to move, stared as it stamped circle-wise over bread and jelly, custard and cress. Colin was somehow expecting Mr Grady to bring down the poker and end this painful and ludicrous situation — in which the hen looked like beating them at last.

It fell dead in the salad, greenery dwarfed by snowing feathers and flecks of blood. The table was wrecked, and the reality of his ruined, hard-earned tea-party reached Mr Grady's sensitive spot. His big face turned red, after the whiteness of shock and superstitious horror. He fixed his wild eyes on Dave, who drew back, treading into his brothers' ankles.

"You bastards," Grady roared, poker still in hand and watched by all. "You bastards, you!"

"I'd like my chicken back," Dave said, as calmly as the sight of Grady's face and shattered table allowed.

Bert and Colin said nothing. Dave's impetuous thieving had never brought them anything but trouble, as far as they could remember — now that things had gone wrong. All this trouble out of one chicken.

Grady girded himself for the just answer: "It's *my* chicken now," he said, trying to smile over it.

"It ain't," Dave said, obstinate.

"You sent it in on purpose," Grady cried, half tearful again, his great chest heaving. "I know you lot, by God I do. Anything for devilment."

"I'd like it back."

Grady's eyes narrowed, the poker higher. "Get away from my house."

"I'm not going till I've got my chicken."

"Get out." He saw Dave's mouth about to open in further argument, but Grady was set on the ultimate word — or at least the last one that mattered, under the circumstances. He brought the poker down on the dead chicken, cracking the salad bowl, a gasp from everyone in the room, including the three brothers. "You should keep your animals under control," he raved. "I'm having this. Now put yourselves on the right side of my doorstep or I'll split every single head of you."

That final thump of the poker set the full stop on all of them, as if the deathblow had been Grady's and gave him the last and absolute right over it. They retreated. What else could you do in face of such barbarity? Grady had always had that sort of reputation. It would henceforth stick with him, and he deserved it more than ever. They would treat him accordingly.

Dave couldn't get over his defeat and humiliation — and his loss that was all the more bitter since the hen had come to him so easily. On their way to the back door he was crying: "I'll get that fat bleeding navvy. What a trick to play on somebody who lives in the same yard! I'll get the bastard. He'll pay for that chicken. By God he will. He's robbed a man of his dinner. He won't get away with a thing like that."

But they were really thinking about what they were going to say to their mother, who had stayed in the house, and who would no doubt remind them for the next few weeks that there was some justice left in the world, and that for the time being it was quite rightly on the side of Mr Grady.

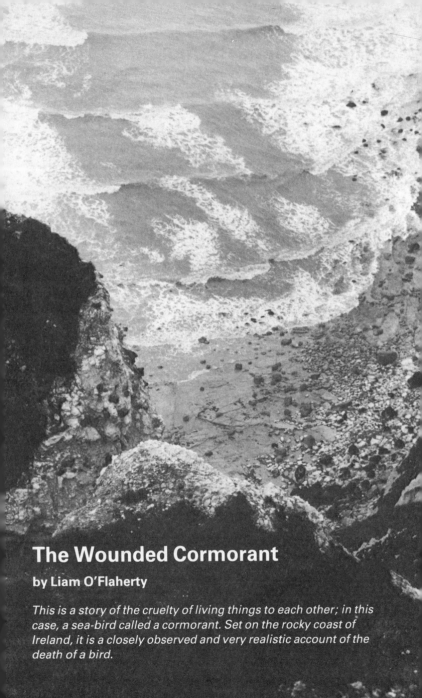

The Wounded Cormorant

by Liam O'Flaherty

This is a story of the cruelty of living things to each other; in this case, a sea-bird called a cormorant. Set on the rocky coast of Ireland, it is a closely observed and very realistic account of the death of a bird.

The Wounded Cormorant

Beneath the great grey cliff of Clogher Mor there was a massive square black rock, dotted with white limpets, sitting in the sea. The sea rose and fell about it frothing. Rising, the sea hoisted the seaweed that grew along the rock's rims until the long red winding strands spread like streams of blood through the white foam. Falling, the tide sucked the strands down taut from their bulbous roots.

Silence. It was noon. The sea was calm. Rock-birds slept on its surface, their beaks resting on their fat white breasts. Tall seagulls standing on one leg dozed high up in the ledges of the cliff. On the great rock there was a flock of black cormorants resting, bobbing their long necks to draw the food from their swollen gullets.

Above on the cliff-top a yellow goat was looking down into the sea. She suddenly took fright. She snorted and turned towards the crag at a smart run. Turning, her hoof loosed a flat stone from the cliff's edge. The stone fell, whirling, on to the rock where the cormorants rested. It fell among them with a crash and arose in fragments. The birds swooped into the air. As they rose a fragment of the stone struck one of them in the right leg. The leg was broken. The wounded bird uttered a shrill scream and dropped the leg. As the bird flew outwards from the rock the leg dangled crookedly.

The flock of cormorants did not fly far. As soon as they passed the edge of the rock they dived headlong into the sea. Their long black bodies, with outstretched necks, passed rapidly beneath the surface of the waves, a long way, before they rose again, shaking the brine from their heads. Then they sat in the sea, their black backs shimmering in the sunlight, their pale brown throats thrust forward, their tiny heads poised on their curved long necks. They sat watching, like upright snakes, trying to discover whether there were any enemies near. Seeing nothing, they began to cackle and flutter their feathers.

But the wounded one rushed about in the water flapping its wings in agony. The salt brine stung the wound, and it could not stand still. After a few moments it rose from the sea and set off at a terrific rate, flying along the face of the cliff, mad with pain. It circled the face of the cliff three times, flying in enormous arcs, as if it were trying to flee from the pain in its leg. Then it swooped down again towards the flock and alighted in the water beside them.

The other birds noticed it and began to cackle. It swam close to one bird, but that bird shrieked and darted away from it. It approached another bird, and that bird prodded it viciously with its beak. Then all the birds screamed simultaneously and rose from the water, with a great swish of their long wings. The wounded one rose with them. They flew up to the rock again and alighted on it, bobbing their necks anxiously and peering in all directions, still slightly terrified by the stone that had fallen there. The wounded one alighted on the rocks with them, tried to stand up, and immediately fell on its stomach. But it struggled up again and stood on its unwounded leg.

The other birds, having assured themselves that there was no enemy near, began to look at the wounded one suspiciously. It had its eyes closed, and it was wobbling unstably on its leg. They saw the wounded leg hanging crookedly from its belly and its wings trailing slightly. They began to make curious screaming noises. One bird trotted over to the wounded one and pecked at it. The wounded bird uttered a low scream and fell forward on its chest. It spread out its wings, turned up its beak, and opened it out wide, like a young bird in a nest demanding food.

Immediately the whole flock raised a cackle again and took to their wings. They flew out to sea, high up in the air. The wounded bird struggled up and also took flight after them. But they were far ahead of it, and it could not catch up with them on account of its waning strength. However, they soon wheeled inwards towards the cliff, and it wheeled in after them, all flying low over the water's surface. Then the flock rose slowly, fighting the air fiercely with their long thin wings in order to propel their heavy bodies upwards. They flew half-way up the face of the cliff and alighted on a wide ledge that was dotted with little black pools and white feathers strewn about.

The wounded bird tried to rise too, but it had not gone out to sea far enough in its swoop. Therefore it had not gathered sufficient speed to carry it up to the ledge. It breasted the cliff ten yards below the ledge, and being unable to rise upwards by banking, it had to wheel outwards again, cackling wildly. It flew out very far, descending to the surface of the sea until the tips of its wings touched the water. Then it wheeled inwards once more, rising gradually, making a tremendous effort to gather enough speed to take it to the ledge where its comrades rested. At all costs it must reach them or perish. Cast out from the flock, death was certain. Seagulls would devour it.

When the other birds saw it coming towards them and heard the sharp whirring of its wings as it rose strongly, they began to cackle fiercely, and came in a close line to the brink of the ledge, darting their beaks forward and shivering. The approaching bird cackled also and came headlong at them. It flopped on to the ledge over their backs and screamed, lying on the rock helplessly with its wings spread out, quite exhausted. But they had no mercy. They fell upon it fiercely, tearing at its body with their beaks, plucking out its black feathers and rooting it about with their feet. It struggled madly to creep in farther on the ledge, trying to get into a dark crevice in the cliff to hide, but they dragged it back again and pushed it towards the brink of the ledge. One bird prodded its right eye with its beak. Another gripped the broken leg firmly in its beak and tore at it.

At last the wounded bird lay on its side and began to tremble, offering no resistance to their attacks. Then they cackled loudly, and, dragging it to the brink of the ledge, they hurled it down. It fell, fluttering feebly through the air, slowly descending, turning round and round, closing and opening its wings, until it reached the sea.

Then it fluttered its wings twice and lay still. An advancing wave dashed it against the side of the black rock and then it disappeared, sucked down among the seaweed strands.

All Things Come of Age
by Liam O'Flaherty

Most stories with animals in them try to make the animals into people. Here is a writer who makes it possible for us to share the experience of an animal realistically, and to sense in what way those experiences are the same and yet are very different from those of human beings.

All Things Come of Age

The baby rabbit was sitting in the sun just by the entrance to his burrow. He was half asleep. His big ears sloped along his back and his sides heaved gently with his breathing. Now and again a slight breeze came up from the stream, raised the brown fur on his side and made silver furrows in it. When the breeze touched him he sniffed the air and wanted his mother to come and feed him.

He was now big enough to graze for his own food along the fertile bank of the stream, but all his brothers and sisters had been killed by a weasel and for that reason there was still enough milk in his mother's drying udder to feed him. So he had not yet been forced to pluck the short blades of grass with his teeth and chew them. All he did was to come out of his burrow, hop about in the sun, smelling the ground, or sit attentively listening to sound, until something menacing came to his ears and he dived into his burrow for shelter.

At the moment, there was perfect peace by the bank of the stream. The sun was still at its height, although it was long past noon. It shone full on the waterfall, that poured with a wild, sad murmur from a narrow gorge, lined with a thick growth of flowering heather. Like a widespread horse's mane, the water poured from the gorge, thick and brown at its base, where it was coloured by the earth and heather and then, falling, it widened out into a silver sheet. There was a long, deep pool below the fall. Flies skimmed its surface and trout leaped at their gaudy wings. At the near end of the pool, just beneath where the little rabbit dozed, there was a line of boulders thrown across the stream. A wild duck stood on one leg in a hollow between two of the boulders. The duck was asleep, with its bill tucked under one wing.

All was still, except for the drowsy music of the waterfall. Some time ago, when the duck swooped down, quacking, onto the boulders, the little rabbit had taken fright and darted into his burrow. But when he peered out again and watched the duck for a long time, as it fed in the stream, prodding with its beak, he became used to the bird and feared it no more. Now it was asleep and it had become part of the surroundings. There was nothing to be seen of it between the boulders, except its flashing wing feathers and a little of its yellow beak.

Suddenly the duck awoke and withdrew its bill from beneath its wing. It raised its neck and turned its head from side to side, listening. Then it began to bob its head and put both feet on the ground. It moved a little to one side, jerking its head and its tail. Then it quacked. It was a low quack, scarcely audible, but it startled the little rabbit. He became wide awake and moved. At first he laid his ears flat along his back and bent down low to the earth on his stomach. Then he raised himself gradually, thrust forward his ears and listened. He watched the duck.

Now the duck was very excited and began to quack continuously. Shaking its gullet, it paddled about on the boulder, taking tiny steps. The little rabbit became very curious, because he failed to discover the cause of the bird's unrest. There was neither sound nor smell. He raised himself on his haunches, thrust his ears as far forward as he could and let his forelegs drop along his breast. He listened and watched intently. He began to get afraid.

Then the duck uttered a loud quack and swept from the boulders with a great swishing of its wings. It swung in a half circle and then shot upwards into the sky, gathering speed as it rose, until it disappeared over a clump of trees farther down the bank of the stream. The rabbit dropped his forelegs to the ground and gathered himself together to make a dive into his burrow. Yet he did not move. The swoop of the duck and the loud swishing of its wings had so startled him that he could not move. So he remained where he was, crouching.

And then, as he lay crouching, he began to feel afraid. It was the same feeling he experienced a few days previously, when his last remaining brother, having hopped into the clump of briars on the left, had suddenly begun to scream. There was a strange feeling in the air, the nearness of a sinister force, that prevented movement. At that time, however, he had been able to move after a little while and run into his burrow. Now it was different.

The sinister feeling increased. There was absolute silence and there was nothing strange to smell and yet he felt the approach of the sinister force, something unknown and monstrous. In spite of himself, although he wanted awfully to hide from it, he looked in the direction whence he sensed the approach of the enemy. His head shook violently as he glanced towards the boulders that lay across the stream. And then he began to scream. A weasel was crossing the line of boulders.

The baby rabbit had never before seen a weasel, but the long brown body, that moved with awful speed, making no sound, drove him crazy with horror. The weasel paused in the middle of the stream, raised his powerful head and stared at the rabbit, his wicked eyes fixed. And then, keeping his head raised and his eyes on his prey, he glided like a flash to the bank. He disappeared for a fraction of a second behind a stone in his path and then appeared again, standing against the little stone, staring fixedly. Now his powerful head, raised above the long brown barrel of his body, was like the boss of a hammer, poised to strike. The rabbit's screaming became wilder. He was now completely in the brute's power, mesmerised by the staring eyes and by the sinister presence.

The weasel, having mesmerised his prey, was on the point of gliding forward to his meal of blood, when the baby rabbit's mother dashed from the clump of briars on the left, screaming as she ran. She moved in a strange fashion, leaping sideways like a dog trying to sight a hare in a field of corn. It was a grotesque dance, to the accompaniment of wild screams. She passed directly in front of the weasel and circled him twice, threatening him each time with her upraised paws. She drew his eyes from her little one towards herself. When they were fixed on her, she dropped to the ground and began to tremble. She crawled away slowly towards the clump of briars, continuing the while to scream. Then she lay down. The weasel slid from the stone and moved towards her swiftly.

As soon as the weasel's eyes left him, the baby rabbit stopped screaming. Then he began to crawl away upstream. He moved as if his back were hurt. He was almost paralysed and it hurt him terribly to draw his hind legs up under his belly in order to hop forward. But the farther away he went from the weasel, the lesser grew the pain in his joints, until at last it seemed that a weight was lifted from his body and he was able to run, staggering a little, into a great hummock of grass that grew around a gorse bush. He bored a bole through the long, coarse grass with his claws and then lay still in the very middle of it, panting. There he fell asleep.

When he awoke it was late in the evening and the sun had set. He felt very hungry. By now, his paroxysm of fear and the weasel's staring eyes were only a vague memory. He wanted to suck his mother and satisfy his hunger. He backed out of his lair in the grass to look for her. He would find her in the burrow where she always fed him in the evening.

He ran back to the burrow as fast as he could, the little white button of his tail hopping as he ran in the twilight like a ball of cotton carried on the wind. He dived eagerly into the burrow and searched for her. The burrow was empty. He came out again, sat on his haunches and raised his ears, smelling and listening. In the distance, frogs were croaking in a marsh. A curlew called on the wing. A multitude of other birds, about to perch for the night, were warbling. He dropped his forelegs and hopped about, smelling the ground, now and again thrusting forward one ear and then another listening. All round the mouth of the burrow, among the thrown out earth, that was pebbled with round droppings, he could smell her, but the smell was old and faint. He went farther from the hole, nosing the ground, in search of a fresher scent.

At last he found one, the track on which she had danced before the weasel. He followed it carefully, round and round, until he came to her, over near the clump of briars. She was lying on her side, already stiff in death. Her udder was towards him and he was on the point of thrusting at the nearest teat with his snout, when he drew back slightly, astonished at the unusual odour which her body exuded. He crouched, with his head close into his neck. Then he thrust forward his head once more timidly, and gently smelt her, all along her body. Just beneath her ear the smell was very strange and terrifying. There was a little hole there and the rim of the hole was clotted with dried blood. As soon as he sniffed the blood, the paroxysm of fear returned. He leaped backwards, sat up on his hind legs, stared at the corpse, squealed and fled to his burrow. He lay in the innermost corner of it, panting.

For a long time he lay there, his head pressed hard against the cold earth. Then again, hunger began to gnaw at his bowels. His hunger gradually became stronger than his fear, driving out the memory of the horrid, clotted blood, around the hole beneath his mother's ear. He forgot his mother. His hunger grew fierce, drowning memory. He crawled out of the burrow.

Night had now fallen and the moon was out, gilding the grassy slope with a fairy light. Several rabbits from neighbouring burrows were grazing in the moonlight. Two little ones, about his own age, were chasing one another. He hopped over to them and began to nibble at the grass.

Dew was now falling on the grass, making it juicy and sweet, just like his mother's milk. When he had eaten his fill, he joined in the dance of the other little rabbits. Now he was no longer afraid and he had completely forgotten his mother. He was one of the herd.

Last Rabbit

by James Cunningham

*We don't know his name, but he's an old man
now living with his daughter and her family. They
have their busy lives to lead, and his daughter has
no time or patience for his dog, Meg. Meg is also
old, and years ago, when he used a dog to help
him shoot rabbits, he would have changed her for
a younger dog. What will he do with her now?*

Last Rabbit

It was morning again and he should be thankful for that he supposed. At his age the old joke wasn't so funny. One day he might just wake up and find himself... Well, not this morning anyway. The world would go on for one more revolution at least.

Downstairs he could hear the sounds of the new day starting. His grandchildren were squabbling over who should feed their pet rabbit. He had given them that. And he could hear their mother's voice, his daughter, and he remembered when Jenny was their age and had a rabbit, too. A big one it had been, black and white, with a queer taste for tea leaves and brown bread crusts.

It was funny. He could remember things like that quite clearly, but sometimes the day before seemed remote and even unimportant.

His daughter was speaking just loud enough for him to hear. Maybe in a voice he was meant to hear, and he pulled himself back from his memory to listen.

He caught the phrase "too old", and then the angry banging of a pot on the stove drowned the rest of the sentence. The only other words he heard were "nuisance" and "not worth wasting food on" before the kitchen door was closed.

For just a moment he thought she had been talking about him. But it was Meg she had meant. Meg, his spaniel; and his hand reached out behind him in the bed till he remembered that Jenny didn't like animals in bedrooms, or in the house much for that matter. Meg slept now in an outhouse.

She was old, he knew that. If he had still been going out with a gun she would have been replaced with a younger dog. No sentimentality; just a pat on the head as thanks for a lifetime's work and then the merciful bullet.

But they had retired together and she was five years past her prime, a long time in a dog's life — and in an old man's. They had grown older together, and deafer, and stiffer. She still kept to his heel on walks in the village and the nearer wood. Only now he carried a stick to help him on the steeper parts, not a gun.

He still had his gun, cased in canvas and leather and oiled against need, though he knew he would never now look along those barrels at a high-flying bird. Sometimes he took it out, to make sure there was no rust, he told himself, and threw it to his shoulder, pleased to see there was no tremble in his arm. And he would run his hand comfortingly over the smoothness of the stock.

He could hear his daughter again, calling him to breakfast. When he got downstairs the children were leaving for school. They had accepted him when he came to stay as they accepted most things in the adult world, without any great enthusiasm. They liked him well enough, he knew, but he wasn't important in their lives. Not as important as that rabbit, nor as necessary as the driver of the bus hooting at the road end waiting to take them to the village school.

They left in a rush, shouting goodbyes and banging the door, and the old man and his daughter sat down at the table. "Look at the mess," she said irritably, pushing aside the dirty plates and brushing ineffectually at the crumbs and spilled marmalade on the tablecloth.

The old man said nothing in reply. At first he had felt obliged to be appeasing in the face of her annoyance but he had learned, or remembered rather from her girlhood, that silence or a diversion was a better answer to her moods.

"Where's Tom?" he asked, after a pause.

"Out to get a breath of fresh air before he goes to work."

He liked his son-in-law. From the beginning Tom had called him Pop; Jenny called him father, or grandpa when the children were about. But Pop was better; it lessened the difference in their ages. Tom talked to him in the evenings, often about things the old man didn't understand, but he pretended interest to keep the conversation going.

"Have you finished?" Jenny asked.

"Yes, thank you. I think I'll follow Tom's example and take a walk this morning. It seems a nice dry day."

His daughter made no reply to this. Instead, like someone who has long had need for speech but given little thought to the words, she burst out: "That dog of yours barked all night. I know you're fond of it, but all night, right below my window. Can't you do anything to keep it quiet?"

"I never heard her," said the old man. "But I'm very sorry." He didn't say that she never barked when she was curled up at

111

the small of his back, and sharing his bed as she shared the rest of his life. "I'll go round and see her."

He drew back the bolt and opened the outhouse door. "Right, lass," he said. Meg rose from her bed of straw and stretched, then came to him. He put his hand down and she touched it with her nose, and they moved off together. At the garden gate the old man stopped and looked down at Meg. She waited to see what he would do, and sat down when he didn't move immediately. Yes, she was old. Her grey muzzle gave her away, but her black and white coat was still silky, her eyes bright, and he had made sure she never became fat.

"You're as fit as I am, lass," he thought. Then aloud he said: "Let's see if we can find a rabbit." He took one step, snapping his fingers for Meg to follow, and stopped again. Meg looked at him doubtfully, for he didn't usually change his mind.

"Wait," he told her. He went back to the house and up to his bedroom, unseen by his daughter washing the dishes in the kitchen. At the back of the cupboard, behind his suits, old-fashioned like himself but serviceable, his shotgun was propped. He took it quickly from its case, put a handful of cartridges in his jacket pocket, and walked back to Meg. At the sight of the gun her stumpy tail began to wag and she gave a few excited yelps.

"Now, lass," was all the man said, and Meg crept silent to his heel. Only her quivering tail showed she knew it was a working day at last.

They took the path to the wood, a popular place at weekends but empty now. Their practised movements made little disturbance to the secret life of the glades they walked through. They were a team, starting again to do the job they were best at.

The trees thinned out after a while and the wood opened into a clearing where the grass, cropped close by rabbits, was gradually being encroached on by bracken. Here the old man sat down, his back against a tree. In the old days there would have been no need for a rest, indeed not even the thought of it. But the day was sunny, and the climb had been steep, and anyway there was no hurry.

He recalled other shooting days with Meg, and with Bess and Spot before her. It had been pheasants and snipe in those days, and duck. Spot had been able to mark and find any duck whether it fell on land or water; a mouth so soft you would have thought his teeth were covered in velvet — except when he ate his dinner, and the old man smiled at the recollection. But Meg was a good dog too. With one finger he scratched the head that was stretched along his knee. They all had their own ways. Meg's was to find game like a pointer and wait till he came up behind her before flushing it.

"Come on, lass. Find me a rabbit." The old man had to put a hand on the tree trunk behind him to steady himself as he got to his feet. Meg watched his moves carefully; this was business.

He broke open the gun and looked along the barrels, then slipped two red cartridges into the breach. He glanced round him, the spot was deserted, and waved his arm forward in a semicircle. He had neither need nor desire for words; Meg understand well enough. She trotted forward a dozen yards and turned to look back at him. He swept his arm to the left and Meg moved in that direction, nose to the ground, to start her hunt for scent.

She still had a good nose. It was her legs that gave her trouble. After that last day's real shooting some years ago they had swelled and he had to nurse her for days until they got better. Today he wouldn't keep her so long. He watched her move up-wind, zigzagging to cover the ground, and shook his head sadly when a rabbit to her right scuttled into cover. At one time she would have seen or heard it, and moved in to let him know where it was. The old man could have shot it from where he stood, but it would have interrupted Meg's stalk and he wanted her to concentrate.

Now Meg was on to one herself. She sank lower to the ground, neck stretched, and stepped forward slowly and precisely, not moving one paw till the other three were secure and silent on the grass. The rabbit, a young one, was nibbling fresh clover leaves on the far side of a bracken patch. Meg knew exactly the point where its doubt would turn to certainty and flight, and she stopped. The old man could not see this rabbit. He followed Meg's path, not as carefully nor as quietly as she had done, but quietly enough. It was important that this rabbit should not move.

When he was close behind Meg he stopped and eased his gun forward. Meg never moved; her mind and body were totally directed at the quarry ahead. Not even her old legs trembled with the strain of staying rigid in one position. She was a machine again until her job was done. This was the life she was trained for, the only life she knew.

The old man looked down at her. She was at her best in action. Idleness and infirmities upset her.

Now the old man moved fast. He shook his head once to clear his thoughts, or perhaps his eyes. Then in one movement he cocked his gun, put the muzzle to the back of Meg's head, and pulled the trigger.

The noise, echoed by the wood, was louder that the old man expected. For a moment the birdsong was stilled, until it broke out again in the alarm clamour. The rabbit on the other side of the bracken leapt for its burrow.

The old man at the same time seemed to be diminished and exalted, older yet prouder. He stepped back, opening the breech of the gun. The spent cartridge was ejected and lay where it fell. The unused cartridge in the other barrel came only half-way out.

With a forefinger the old man rubbed the brass end. At his touch it slid invitingly back into the breech. He looked at one barrel end, blackened and still with pale blue smoke curling out of it, then at the other, closed with bright brass. He closed the gun again, slowly. And then quickly snapped it open. This time the unused cartridge fell on to the grass.

He put it in his pocket and turned for home. He would have to ask Jenny if he could borrow Tom's spade.

Meima-Bucha

by Ruth Fainlight

A young girl is taken by her mother to visit an elderly Jewish woman, Meima-Bucha. The old woman is in a sad situation, living in poor accommodation in a depressed part of the city of New York; her children have grown up and rarely see her; she is poor, ill, and not well looked after. What does the young girl feel towards her?

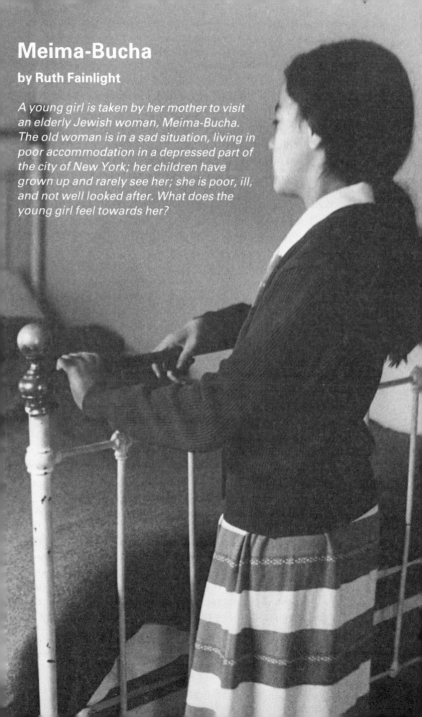

Meima-Bucha

I remembered an old woman called Meima-Bucha. I have forgotten her exact relationship; I think she was a great-aunt. Her children were grown up and absorbed by their own lives in various New York suburbs, and perhaps somewhat ashamed of her. An invalid now, she still lived in two tenement[1] rooms in the same district where she had first settled on arrival in the country, her only companion being another woman hired by her family to look after her. Whenever my mother or my aunt went to the city they would go to see Meima-Bucha. During the summer I was eleven my mother took me for one of these visits.

We travelled by elevated train in an almost empty car. It was a hot, dry day in early August, and sun, coming through the dust-smeared windows, lit the seats to a bright, ripe banana yellow. I sat quietly, hypnotised by the small hexagonal patterns of woven straw until it was time to get off.

My mother and I walked down the iron steps from the littered station into the street below, full of delicatessens, dry cleaners, and drug stores. The top had been taken off a hydrant, and a cluster of small children ran screaming and naked into the spray. We crossed an empty and dirty boulevard. Opposite was a large vacant lot, the earth dried into a fine, grey-brown dust, on which stood a few garbage cans and a large, solitary billboard advertising some brand of gasoline.

Rows of tall, dull brown buildings began again, and very hot by now, we trudged past four or five before entering a high open door on one side of which was a row of bells, and besides each bell an empty, rusted nameplate container.

After the glaring asphalt sidewalk the hallway seemed a cold and musty cavern. But my mother knew the way. There were eight floors to these buildings. We climbed more and more slowly through smells of grey soapy mops and the pungent meals of all the families who had ever lived in the rooms we were passing, until we reached the fifth landing and Meima-Bucha's door.

[1] *tenement*: a set of apartments; usually poor rented accommodation

My mother knocked, and in a few moments the woman who lived with Meima-Bucha looked distrustfully out through a narrow opening. She was a thin hunchback of about fifty-five with a tight, olive-coloured face, dressed in an ankle-length dark cotton dress covered by a dark printed apron.

"Hello, Yetta," my mother said. "How is she?"

"Not too good," the woman answered. Her voice sounded strange, as if she used English rarely. "Come on, I'll take you in to her."

She led my mother through a small, windowless room into the next where Meima-Bucha lay, staring out all day across the airshaft to the wall of windows opposite.

I lingered, curious to examine everything. In one corner stood a large, old-fashioned black iron stove with a flue pipe leading up to the murkiness of the ceiling. Behind the door was a small bed covered with a grey woollen blanket, and against the other wall a dark-stained wooden chest of drawers. Having exhausted the room's possibilities, I joined the others.

As I passed the little hunchback standing like a sentinel inside the door Meima-Bucha lifted her head, for she was not completely paralysed. She lay on a high iron bed, dressed in a soiled flannel nightgown open at the throat, revealing the loose wrinkled skin of her neck and her dull-fleshed chest. White hair stuck out all around her head, and she was crying. When her milky-grey eyes saw me, her sobs increased. I stood close to my mother, embarrassed by Meima-Bucha's helplessness, and awkwardly said,

"Hello, how are you?"

But Meima-Bucha could not understand English; all her life she had spoken only Yiddish[1]; and tears continued to flow down her face.

"Kiss her," my mother murmured, nudging me.

I bent and kissed her cheek. She was over seventy, and never visited by her children, but I felt that she had almost forgotten them and did not weep now for any reason, not even self-pity, but only because she was old.

My mother touched her shoulder and she took my hand and blessed me, then turned away to continue their soft, quick conversation. Unable to move without disturbing her, I tried to

---

[1] *Yiddish*: language spoken by Jewish community; a mixture of an old form of German and many modern words

guess what she was saying. After a while she dropped my hand and reached for my mother's. I walked to the window and looked out, down the five storeys, through angled lines of washing to the yard below. A few children were playing there, transformed by steep perspective into heads and feet, and I followed their game from my vantage point. Then I turned back to the room.

The smell of bedclothes and sickness oppressed me. The hunchbacked woman, still standing by the door, glanced fiercely over, sensing my boredom. I looked down at my striped cotton skirt and pleated it between my fingers, then moved to my mother's chair and leaned against it, lulled by the unintelligible conversation.

At last my mother stood up. She kissed Meima-Bucha, almost crying herself, and put her arm around my shoulder, to bring me close for my farewell. The old woman realised we were leaving and wept bitterly, now having an object in her tears. Her wet mouth, the tears on my face, my mother's strangeness — transformed as she seemed by another language — made me desperate to get out. After another kiss my mother walked into the next room, followed by myself and the hunchback.

"Here, take this to buy her a new nightgown," my mother said, pushing some bills into the woman's hands. She accepted the money without comment.

"You know, she's not clean; you really ought to look after her better," my mother added sharply.

The women assured my mother she did her best. There was nothing else to say and nothing possible to do, so we left. Meima-Bucha's companion hung over the banisters watching us until we reached the ground floor.

The streets that had seemed so unpleasant before were now fresh, light, and sweet-smelling. My mother walked thoughtfully by my side.

"You see how awful it is when you're old, and your children leave you," she said. "Poor old Meima-Bucha. It's shameful."

But I did not understand what she meant, and could only feel my horror at the old woman.

Some years later Meima-Bucha died. When I read of her death in a letter from my aunt, I remembered my feelings of disgust and fear. My aunt added that Meima-Bucha's children had given her a magnificent funeral.

Hurricane Season

by Edgar Mittelholzer

Hurricanes are a hazard to be feared in Barbados, but this story is more about old age than the hurricane; indeed, the hurricane that old Jacob Everett fears doesn't actually come! We learn about Jacob, his wife, and his son, Francis, from the evening when a hurricane was feared.

Hurricane Season

Since early morning the air had been calm, oppressive, and the wind, whenever it did blow, seemed to come from all directions at once. It came in hot, brief gusts, as though afraid to commit itself, or as though it were the breath of some monster whose throat were being pressed open at jerky intervals by a giant thumb. The sea, under the overcast sky, pounded continously on the pebbly beach, hoarse and angry, one breaker curling high and crested after the other in quick succession. The white pebbles of coral that strewed the beach clicked and rattled as the hissing foam rushed furiously over them.

Old Jacob Everett had lit a fire so that he could watch the smoke and tell how the wind was blowing. The smoke kept whisking this way and that, a purposeless ghost that often would insinuate itself into the rickety, two-roomed hut and cause Mother Everett to cough. Whenever it did this Mother Everett would put her head out of the tiny window of the back room and scold her husband — scold him in a voice that lacked confidence, for she had long resigned herself to the fact that he was a self-willed man upon whom scoldings had no effect.

"Why you don't come insoide, ole man? Is what you t'ink you doing? You can't stop God's works..."

"Ole fishermen loike you so 'fraid de wedder. Shame 'pon you, Jacob! You doting too bad in you' ole age! Ef hurricane come tonoight it's de will of Jehovah. Put out de fire. De smoke choking up me pore lungs."

Everett, as usual, took no notice. He kept the fire going with odd pieces of anything he collected along the seashore. Coconut branches the sea had washed up and half-buried in the sand, seaweed dried crisp by the sun, twigs and dead leaves from under the sea-grape trees and the manchineels[1] and tall casuarinas[2] that lined the shore, coconut shells and even an old boot.

---

[1] *manchineels:* a tree, common in the West Indies, with poisonous sap and a fruit that looks like an apple, but is very sour
[2] *casuarinas:* a tree, so called because its branches look like the feathers of birds

As he watched the smoke, which sometimes would be grey-blue and sometimes dark brown, the tint of his troubled face, he shook his head and mumbled to himself that it looked bad. "Dis look very bad."

Every hurricane season — from the beginning of July to the end of September — for the past three years, he had suffered from this fear, and Mother Everett blamed it on two things — "ole age doting" and Francis.

Francis, their youngest son, was a brilliant boy, and with the help of his sister Doris, who had married a schoolteacher, he had got a secondary education, and was now a teacher himself. He came often to the fishing village to see his parents, but Mother Everett said half-jokingly that it was an evil day when he had brought "dat big black book some few years back".

The big black book she meant was one of a pile Francis had been taking home with him; he lived with Doris and her husband farther along the coast. He had just come from the Public Library in Bridgetown, six miles away, and his father had said proudly: "Well, look dis! Boy, you mean tell we you studying all dem big books? Heh!" And Mother Everett had grunted and said between sucks at her clay pipe: "Dis island o' Barbados na able hold Francis when he done study all dem books, you hear what Oi says, Jacob." And then Francis, embarrassed and trying to be modest, had changed the subject by remarking: "Something in this one moight interest you, Papa. Remember we used to talk about hurricanes and how Barbados never had one for more than a hundred years? Well, this book is a history of Barbados. A man called Schomburgk wrote it, and it describe the two biggest hurricanes we ever had here. Long, long time ago. One happen in 1780 and the other in 1831."

Francis had read aloud for them the vivid accounts of the two great hurricanes, and old Everett had nodded and groaned and grunted, absorbed and deeply impressed ... "Red sky. Yes. Oh, yes. Oi always did hear say red sky mean trouble in de heavens. My fadder tell me so plenty toime."

But Mother Everett had laughed. "All you fishermen, you always says dat! Red sky mean rain and t'under-lightning. How much red sky me ain' see since I was a girl and no rain and t'under-lightning come — much less hurricane!"

But Everett never forgot what Francis had read from the history book.

"See how de wind blow," he muttered to himself, watching the smoke this day in August. "Dis way now, dat way now. Variable, de word mean, and it was the very word de book use. Variable. Same as de big book Francis read from say. Francis tell me what wind blow variable in 1831, de day before de big hurricane break. And it was a August day loike today wid de sea rough and de sky overcast. Yes, dis look bad. Dis look very bad."

His gaze shifted over to the hut, and took note, perhaps for the fifth or sixth time that day, of its condition. The shingles[1] he had nailed to the walls more than thirty years ago were grey and ragged at the edges; some of them were askew, some falling out. On the roof the corrugated iron was a red-brown hue — the colour of the shingles when they had been new. But this red-brown was the red-brown of rust. At night before he fell asleep he would listen to sections of the corrugated iron flapping screechily in the wind. It leaked in two or three places. He had stopped leaks more times than he could count during the past ten years.

In his fancy he could see the whole flimsy structure toppling off its foundation of coralline limestone blocks, could see the waves — waves twenty feet high — smashing down upon the rotten walls from which cockroaches and centipedes scurried. The history book from which Francis had read had said that during a hurricane the sea rose and pounded the beach with huge waves. What hope would there be for this hut if the sea rose and the wind turned into a hundred-mile-an-hour gale!

Somehow, he did not fear death. It was the loss of the hut that worried him. It was the one thing that had always meant security in his life. He and Mother Everett had built it with their own labour and their own tools over thirty years ago when his own parents had been alive. To lose this hut would be to feel as exposed as a snail would feel without its shell.

That was what Mother Everett did not understand. She thought he was afraid for his life. Why should he be when he and his fishing-boat had battled through so many murderous seas and merciless squalls? It was true that now at seventy-one his fishing days were over; Doris and Francis helped him along with an allowance every month, and James and Harry helped,

[1] *shingles:* tiles made of bark, nailed to walls or roofs as weather proofing

too, when they could; James and Harry, not having clever brains like Francis, had done like their father and become fishermen. Yes, his fishing days were over, but that didn't mean he had turned into a coward. Why, he was even convinced there was no storm that could kill him.

No, it was the hut. "Dis hut," he muttered, turning his gaze out upon the sea. The waves had a purplish-grey tint under the dull sky. Yesterday, in the sunshine, they had looked such a bright, cheerful blue ... "What we will do if dis hut get smash up?"

As the afternoon progressed the sky became blacker, and in the south and south-east thunder muttered frequently. Hurricanes always approached from the south or south-east and travelled north-east or north-west.

The wind, after four o'clock, increased in strength and came definitely from a south-easterly direction. Sometimes it veered to the south, but at no time did it come from the north-east. Another bad sign, Everett noted. When the North-East Trades were blowing there was little chance of a hurricane. The Trades brought fine weather.

At five o'clock, rain began to fall in large, coarse drops, and Everett's fire hissed and went out. He retired into the hut for the meal Mother Everett had been calling him since three o'clock to come and eat – two three-cent loaves of bread and a cup of hot water mixed with a teaspoonful of sweetened condensed milk. The third and last meal of the day. This morning at seven it had been exactly the same: two three-cent loaves and a cup of hot water with condensed milk.

As Everett ate he remembered something Mr Franklin, the village grocer, had said a few months ago. Mr Franklin had told a customer he had read in the newspaper that people all over the island were advised to put in a big stock of foodstuffs in July in the event of a hurricane. Old Everett had shaken his head and uttered a moan to himself. Poor people like him could barely find rice and potato and bread and milk from day to day. How could the newspaper advise them to put in a big stock of foodstuffs? That advice was for the rich people: the big sugar planters and the merchants and their families in Bridgetown – and the Civil Servants and the holiday people who came to Barbados. Another piece of advice Mr Franklin said the newspaper gave was that when a hurricane warning was sounded people should board up their windows and doors with good lumber — not just any kind of lumber[1] but good lumber. Old Everett had groaned on hearing this. People like him didn't even have bad lumber, much less good lumber. If he had had lumber of any kind at all he would have used it to repair the hut, not board up windows and doors.

The rain grew fiercer, and drummed loud on the corrugated iron roof. Mother Everett brought an enamel basin from the back room to set down on the floor near the old bamboo table, and the basin at once began to give out sharp ping-pong sounds as the rain leaked into it in slow, big drops.

Everett listened, but he could hear only rain. The wind seemed to have died down.

Mother Everett sat in the rocking-chair, her ragged Bible in her lap. Her lips kept moving as she read. Her sight was perfect. Every afternoon at this time, bad weather or good, she read her Bible. This afternoon she had lit a stump of candle and stood it on the table beside her chair, for with the wooden shutters closed against the rain the hut was as dark as though it were after sundown.

Everett finished his meal, and remained seated on the box that served him as chair — the rocker was the only authentic chair in the hut — staring at the floor and pondering still on the weather. He waved his hand before his face. This heat was another very bad sign. Since early morning — long before the sun had come up — the heat had begun.

Suddenly he glanced up. The rain had stopped — abruptly and ominously. There was still no wind. Why had the wind died away like that?

The sea continued its riotous crashing roar on the beach, and far away he heard a prattling roll of thunder. Rising, he opened the door, and Mother Everett glanced up and said: "You going outside mek more smoke, Jacob? Why you don't stan' insoide, ole man?"

"Going watch de wedder, Susan. It looking bad, girl. Very bad."

"You say dat two weeks back, and nutting happen."

"It wasn't so bad as dis. Today Oi see al de soigns, Susan. Jest as Francis read from dat big book. Hurricane coming for sure tonoight."

Groaning, he went outside.

[1] *lumber:* wood

The sea-grape trees dripped solemnly, and the huge manchineel trees, farther along the beach, looked frowning and threatening, as though thunder were concealed in their dense foliage. They bore poisonous berries. Berries you even had to be careful not to tread on with bare feet, for the juice in them caused illness. As a boy his parents had often warned him to be careful of them... As a boy ... Such a long time ago that was. In 1898 he went on a trip in a schooner as a deck hand. They touched Dominica, St Lucia, Antigua. And when he came back his father, he remembered, told him that a big storm had struck Barbados while he was away. Not a hurricane, but nearly a hurricane. The wind had uprooted a few trees and knocked down some huts here and there. He had been so disappointed that he had been out of the island and had missed the experience. Stupid fool that he was then...

He came to a halt.

The sky in the west and the south was slowly turning a deep crimson. The blue-grey thunder-clouds moving slowly towards the north-west stood cut dramatically against this background of crimson. Large fans of crimson that splayed out upwards to the zenith and that gradually, as he watched, began to infect the thunder-cloud whose edges grew pink and then mauve, and this mauve spread and spread until the very depths of the clouds were aglow with a sombre, regal purplish red.

A gust of wind came puffing from the south-east, hot and making a drone in his ears. But now it was not the wind that troubled him. It was the sky. A red sky.

He sank down on the damp earth and held his head in his hands. Now it was only a matter of waiting. Now he must resign himself and take what was coming. God's works... "You can't stop God's works," Susan had said.

So he waited.

Darkness fell, the crimson fading from the sky. He could hear thunder rumbling in the distance again. From the south-east. Some large drops of rain fell, but only sparsely, and not for long.

The wind died away entirely. The heat increased — and the oppressiveness. The heat seemed like a mesh around him. Mother Everett called twice, but he took no heed. Would not even answer. The heat had him trapped so that whether he had wanted to or not he could not have moved.

He must sit here and wait... God's works...

The sea darkened, and the waves seemed to gather a new

agitation, a new fury, as they thundered down on the beach. He listened to the swishing prattle of the pebbles at each onslaught.

The sky shut down upon the land and the sea, hanging heavier and heavier like a black furry carcase laden with moist death.

He sat without moving. Sleep, after a while, made him nod. And Mother Everett called again and again. But he did not move. He could feel the salty, sticky spray from the sea damp against his face and arms as it billowed across the short stretch of grassy land that separated him from the beach.

He continued to wait, nodding off and on as sleep bore down like the clouds upon him. And after one of these nodding spells — it seemed a long one — he woke and shook his head, and saw that the sea had taken on a phosphorescent look. Each wave came clear and crested through the darkness, glittering blue-green. It was weird. Terrible and weird. At least, it was so until he looked up and saw a half-moon in the sky, inclined to the west. It was the moon, then, that made the waves look phosphorescent.

Funny, he thought, that the moon should be shining. He looked around and saw stars. Scorpio was sinking in the west — not far from the moon. Everywhere he looked there were stars. In the north and in the south and in the east as well as in the west. And the air was very cool.

Behind him the hut was in darkness. Mother Everett must have gone to bed.

He rose and looked around again to make quite sure.

Not a cloud in the sky, except a few wisps low down on the horizon. And the wind seemed to have shifted back to the north-east. The good, kindly, cooling Trade Winds. Portent of fine weather.

Last Love

by Angela Huth

The old people in this story are well looked after
in Sunset Home, a home for old people. Tom and
Beth were both married, but now Tom's wife and
Beth's husband are dead. They develop an
affection for each other, and marry again. Is it
possible to make a life for themselves at their
age?

Last Love

Beth Soper bent her head to avoid seeing the clouds in the sky and set off down the Bermondsey Street to St Michael's Church. There, Thomas Harrow was waiting for her and they were quietly married. Beth was seventy-eight and Thomas was eighty-two.

They had wanted no fuss, just a simple private ceremony. Their friends in the Sunset Home had asked permission to come to the church, eager for an outing. But when they had been refused, they understood. There was promise of some kind of celebration later, after the honeymoon.

Man and wife, Thomas and Beth returned to the street hand in hand. The vicar had offered them a lift in his car, but they said no, they would enjoy the walk. They hadn't gone far when it began to rain.

"Dratted weather," said Thomas.

"My hat," said Beth. With her free hand she patted at the pale blue feathers which were becoming clotted in the wet.

Thomas had not seen the flat furnished, and it seemed to please him. Beth had just managed to get it all ready in time, with the help of Madge and Eileen from the Sunset, and the lady from the Welfare. Beth pointed out every detail to Thomas lest he should miss something: green tiles in the bathroom, nice yellow kitchen curtains, velvet three-piece suite in the sitting-room, patchwork bedspread (one of the few things she had kept when Christopher died). Thomas said he thought it was all grand. He said their savings had been well spent.

When he had seen everything, and repeated his approving comments several times, Beth lit the gas fire and they sat side by side on the sofa, noting with pleasure its firm springs. It was only eleven-thirty, a good hour before Beth should heat up the tin of Swiss ravioli for lunch, but she suggested they should wait no longer to cut the cake. It was a rich fruit cake iced in pink and white. Kept in a tin, it would last for weeks. Beth's daughter Annie had sent it with best wishes from Plymouth.

They ate their slices slowly, to guard against indigestion. After a while Thomas said, "Well, Mrs Harrow, we're married at last."

Beth's head, which of late shook constantly, like a flower in a slight wind, nodded more strongly in agreement. She was thinking that tomorrow she would pay for the rum in Annie's cake, and how she would enjoy the afternoon sorting out their stores in the kitchen cupboard. Her own kitchen again. Strange thought, really, but a good one.

Thomas and Beth met in the Sunset Home. Thomas had been there several years before Beth arrived from a Home in the country. She was newly widowed, and very quiet. From his chair in the semicircle round the television — a long way from the chair assigned to Beth — Thomas observed she was prettier than most of the old ladies who came. She had a kindly face and a lively eye, though of course this was veiled by present sadness, her husband having so recently died.

They did not have occasion to speak for several months. Then one Saturday afternoon, in the middle of 'Match of the Day', the old man in the chair next to Thomas shut his eyes and died. It gave them all a shock. They were used to their neighbours dying, but were upset by the witnessing of actual death. Going into tea that day, the bell ringing imperviously in his ears, Thomas found his mouth trembling and his eyes filled with tears. William Best and he had sat next to each other for seven years. They had not tried to know each other very well, but they enjoyed their mutual silence. They would nod at each other's occasional remarks, and sometimes share a bag of sweets.

In his upset state Thomas hardly noticed a tug at his elbow. It made him sway a little on his feet. Beth Soper it was: the pretty old lady who still looked sad. He struggled to regain his balance.

"Terrible thing, death in the afternoon," she said quietly. "I know how you felt about Mr Best."

"Ah," said Thomas. And then an inspiration came to him. Beth should take William's place. Beth should be his armchair neighbour. "I would like it if you moved into his chair," he said, "otherwise they'll put in a new one. There's no accounting for who I'd get."

Beth thought about it only for a moment. Then she said, "Very well. I'll move my rug after tea."

After that Thomas and Beth stuck closely together. Beth moved into Mr Best's place in the dining-room, too, and by the second meal Thomas knew she liked two spoons of sugar in her tea and put them in without asking. Beth was impressed. He was a good, quiet man, Thomas, but uncared for. It wasn't long before she was darning his socks and reminding him to tie his laces. On Sunday, if it was fine, they would go for a drink together in the local pub. Wednesdays they would walk to the post box: Beth wrote to Annie every Tuesday evening, and Thomas wrote to his son Allan, in Australia, once a month. Neither of them received much news in return, but their mutual reminiscences were some compensation for lack of letters or visitors.

Thomas and Beth's association did not go unobserved by the others, for all its quietness. "The young lovers" they came to be known as, and sometimes blushed at the public ragging. If they left the television room together to repair to the small lounge for a few moment's peace, they would cause much speculation and merriment at supper.

"Young lovers at it again?" Alice, the spinster ringleader, would croak. "You'll be dead before your time, this rate."

Laughter all round, threads of soup wavering down chins. Beth privately thought Alice was coarse — she had been in the fish market all her life, after all — and was uncertain how to react to her jibes. Thomas, sensing the difficulty of Beth's smile, would move his wiry thigh to touch hers under the table, and she would be comforted.

On Christmas Eve Thomas proposed to Beth in the small sink room where they filled their hot water bottles each night. There was no one about. Drip of the tap and growl of the kettle the only noises. Night sky through the curtainless window, milky with reflections from the neon city outside.

"I was thinking it might be more sensible, Beth, if we lived out the rest of our years together as man and wife." He was calm and firm, sure as he had been all those years ago when he had proposed to Josephine O'Reilly on Westminster Bridge.

"Well, that would be nice, I think," said Beth, unscrewing the cap of her hot water bottle.

"Seeing as we're both in such good health we could leave this place, find ourselves a little flat. Be independent."

"So we could," said Beth, and the idea of her own home again made her hand tremble. She returned the kettle to the table for fear of spilling the scalding water.

"We could discuss it more in the morning, when you've had time to sleep on it," went on Thomas, with his usual consideration.

"Oh, I'll say yes all right. There won't be any changing my mind in the night." Beth smiled shyly at him.

"There! You sound like a girl." Thomas handed her a filled bottle, screwed tightly as he could manage with his arthritic hands, and kissed her on the forehead. Then they went their separate ways down the corridor.

Thomas gave Beth a cameo brooch for Christmas; she gave him the pair of red socks she had sworn she was knitting for her son-in-law.

"And what about a ring?" Thomas asked. "An engagement isn't right without a ring."

Beth looked down at the wedding band Christopher Randolph Crest had slipped on her finger in a Dorset church in the spring of 1915, promising to have her and to hold till death parted them, and he had kept that promise. She wouldn't like to take his ring off now, for all that he would be pleased she was to marry again and be happy (a different sort of happy, of course). Besides, it wouldn't be possible to get it off, over her swollen knuckles. Beth felt the brush of one of the small awkwardnesses of second marriage. She fingered her new brooch.

"Oh, not a ring, Thomas," she said. "This is quite enough, what you've given me already. Very like one my mother had. And anyhow ..."

She held out her hands. They looked at the lumpy joints on what had once been long and thin fingers.

"Very well, on this occasion," said Thomas, and lapsed into an understanding silence. Beth was grateful to him.

Their engagement was not a secret for long. Everyone approved of the idea and rejoiced. They sent small presents wrapped in tissue paper: soap and tobacco, writing paper, a potted hyacinth. Madge and Eileen efficiently set about finding a council flat, and on fine days Beth went shopping for things they would need, most of her savings, added to Thomas's, in her bag.

In early spring Beth fell ill. Perhaps it was a chill: a nasty wind unexpectedly had savaged her on one of her shopping expeditions. Perhaps it was all the excitement — no one could tell. The doctor said she would soon recover if she took things quietly for a while. But the wedding, planned for March, had to be postponed.

Beth, in bed, cameo brooch on a velvet ribbon round her neck, cried a little. Thomas sat by her, dabbing her handkerchief with eau de cologne.

"Don't worry yourself," he said.

"But I do, Thomas."

"You just gather your strength."

"I never had more than a day's illness in my life. Christopher said I was strong as an ox."

"We'll be married soon as you're on your feet."

Beth cheered a little. They could hear Alice's penetrating voice in the corridor.

"Expect she's come to see what we're doing," said Beth. "Whatever will she be thinking?"

They both smiled.

It took Beth longer than she had supposed to recover completely. But with the warmth of summer strength returned to her, a new date was set for the wedding in October. By then, the council flat was acquired, the furniture in, the carpets down. The day of the wedding there was early sun. The rain that came later was disappointing, but neither of them really cared. They had too much else to think about: so much to plan for the years ahead.

The first day as Mrs Harrow passed very quickly: there was all the enjoyment of sorting out the kitchen cupboards, of seeing Thomas dozing in an armchair (which soon would lose its new look) in front of his own gas fire − of making mince in a parsley sauce for supper. The sauce was a little lumpy, but Beth felt soon she would be back in practice.

They did not stay up late. When the nine o'clock news was over they took it in turns to undress in the bathroom. Then they lay in the new bed, just touching, the patchwork quilt drawn up high across their chests.

"I think this was a very good idea of mine," said Thomas.

"It was, too." Beth smiled.

"My first honeymoon wasn't half as damn comfortable as this."

"Nor mine," said Beth.

Thomas sighed.

"Ah, Beth, if it was years ago ... a few years ago."

"Put all that out of your mind," said Beth, touching her hairnet.

"You can't help thinking," said Thomas. "Still, I should be grateful for a lively mind, even if the old bones can't keep up with it."

"I should say so," said Beth.

Thomas took her hand.

"Believe me, I was quite ... a devil in my time."

"Of course you were," said Beth. "Now, I'm going to put out the light."

They kissed, briefly, each smelling an echo of parsley sauce and wedding cake on the other's breath. In the dark, their legs intertwined.

For a while they were silent, listening for signals of sleep in the other's breathing: pondering upon the extraordinary sensation of someone new, however much loved, beside them in bed. Then Thomas said,

"Beth, I can't manage to sleep with ... I mean if you don't mind I'd like to take out −"

"There's a glass of water beside your bed, love," said Beth.

"You're a good and thoughtful woman, you know." Beth felt him move, stretch his arm about in the darkness. She heard two small splashes in the water. "Happy marriage doesn't mean changing all one's ways, does it, Beth? That's what Josephine and I agreed."

Then suddenly he was definitely asleep, on his back, snoring a more rattling snore than Christopher Randolph Crest's; but she would get used to it. Beth turned on to her side. Living into old age with someone you scarcely noticed the changes, could not be sure of the precise time when your habits changed, more milk puddings by day, bedsocks and bare gums by night. There was no unease. With a new person the small private acts of an ageing body could cause awkwardness close to shame unless there was much understanding. With Thomas, Beth could not imagine feeling more happily herself, but all the same she was glad that it was dark and he was asleep when she dropped her own teeth into the glass of water at her side of the bed. Then, at once, she joined her husband in sleep.

When she thought about it later Beth could not recall exactly when it was that she began to find running the flat more difficult than she had supposed. Accustomed to the sedentary life in the Sunset, no worries about food and shopping and washing up, she had felt full of energy − indeed fed up, sometimes, that there was not more she could do. Now, with everything to think about again, to be responsible for, she felt curiously tired. Thomas helped as much as he could, of course: he carried the shopping bag and laid the table, but it had always been Beth's belief that it was a wife's duty to look after her husband once he had retired, and she would not allow him to assist her as much as he would have liked. Besides, he was older than her.

Gradually, the punctilious rhythm of the day, which Beth had adhered to all her life, and had expected would continue in her new married life, began to disintegrate. It occurred to her that she and Thomas were still in their dressing gowns at eleven o'clock one morning, and last night's supper things were unwashed in the sink. The pile of clothes to be ironed had grown dauntingly high, and winter sun exposed the dusty tops of furniture. On shopping expeditions the cold bit through their gloves, and made their arthritic hands to ache, and to open a tin, to turn on a tap or do up a button became a struggle. Some days, when it rained and a vicious wind blew, neither Beth nor Thomas had the heart to go out and buy something for supper. They made do with bread and jam, and suffered indigestion the next morning.

Madge and Eileen visited them every now and then: Beth made them tea and bought iced buns with wings of angelica, and listened with interest to news of the Sunset. Madge and Eileen seemed concerned: but Beth and Thomas assured them independent married life was very nice: no troubles, they could not be happier. And indeed this was true: to have your own home, rather than to be part of an institution, however comfortable, was an achievement in old age: and although neither ever mentioned it, both Thomas and Beth privately intended to die at home.

They bought a budgerigar and a collection of cacti for their window, and sometimes they treated themselves to the luxury of a small glass of sherry, or brandy, which they preferred now to drink on their sofa rather than in the pub. They spoke often of their children, and their past, and of the odd characters in the Sunset, and felt quietly content, while all about them gathered signs of Beth's fatigue. Sometimes, she worried so much about what to give Thomas for his lunch or supper that she could not sleep. She was stricken with headaches in the morning. She could no longer make pastry, she discovered, because of her arthritis, and for so long she had been telling Thomas what a good pastry maker she was. He believed her, of course, even though she could produce no proof: but the disappointment depressed her.

Then one morning, the first snow of the year smudging their window, Beth knew she could not get up. A great weakness gripped her, making her too feeble to explain how she felt. Thomas made her a cup of tea, and brought her biscuits for lunch, and she stayed in bed all day.

That night a terrible pain spread over her chest and she moaned out loud. Thomas woke. He took one look at her, dragged on his heavy coat over his pyjamas, and went downstairs to the call box to ring for an ambulance. Beth was taken to hospital. Heart attack, they said.

Madge and Eileen were very good about it all. They assured Thomas that when Beth was better there would be room for the two of them back at the Sunset. Thomas protested. He wanted so much to return to their own flat: he would insist on doing more of the housework, he said, and perhaps a home help could be found. But the doctor was adamant. Beth needed professional care.

And so Thomas moved back to the Sunset, to a new, light room with twin beds. He left it to Madge and Eileen to organise the selling of their new furniture and carpets and curtains. They gave him quite a large cheque, but it gave him no pleasure. He bought roses for Beth, and a pretty shawl, her favourite blue, and a picture of a country village which he hoped would remind her of Dorset. He visited the hospital each day, almost an hour's journey on the bus, and in between visits the hours passed slowly.

Beth returned within ten days, seemingly recovered. But, once again, she had instructions to take things quietly. So they spent most of the day in their room, away from the others with their sympathetic looks. They had their television and their budgerigar, and received much kindness. But for all that, they missed their own flat.

One evening Thomas noticed that Beth's complexion had deepened to the colour of a stormy sky, and her eyes were sad as they had been when he first saw her. She began to talk about their time in the flat, and Thomas realised Beth was a little confused: she thought they had spent many years there. In reality it had been scarcely six weeks.

But Thomas did not contradict her. She seemed happy to talk about their past. In some way it seemed to have replaced the greater stretch of time she had spent with Christopher Randolph Crest, and she wanted Thomas to assure her that when she was quite better they could return to the flat and continue their independent lives.

"It will all be waiting for us, just as we left it," she said. "Just a few weeks' time. A good dust, and there we'll be."

Thomas broke the news to her gently.

"Not that flat, won't," he said. "You see, you being ill, it had to be given up, now we're back here. But we can get another one, just the same. Easy. Same block, probably."

"Oh, good," said Beth. "That will be nice."

"Just a little patience, that's all we need." Thomas found his own mind confused, now: perhaps another flat was a real possibility. Beth, with all her spirit, even after the heart attack, seemed so sure she could manage it. He had faith in her. He was sure she could. He pulled a small package out of his pocket.

"Here," he said.

"Oh, Thomas, you shouldn't." Beth opened it with trembling hands. It was a small porcelain pot encrusted with roses.

"For your hairpins," Thomas said. Beth smiled. She looked beautiful in the evening light, in spite of the glowering colour of her skin.

"You spoil me, you know," she said. "It's just like you're courting me all over again, isn't it?"

Thomas scratched his head.

"Seems to me when we were courting before we were making plans. We got a lot more plans to make again." He could not quite think what they were, but felt a strange certainty that in the days to come, with the return of Beth's health, they would sort themselves out.

Beth pulled her blue shawl more closely round her shoulders. She touched the cameo brooch at her neck, given to her by Thomas Harrow, and the wedding ring on her finger, given to her by Christopher Randolph Crest, and it seemed to her that everybody was together again in the room. They were all rejoined for the future.

"A few days and I'll be out in the shops, looking," she said. "Wait till you see." Her head nodded at the darkening sky. "I'm a little tired tonight, I think, but tomorrow we'll make a list of what we'll need ... Thomas Christopher," she added, "you're good to me."

Thomas patted her hand. He was glad that she had put his

name first, and that she agreed with him about what they should do, and that they were married. He heard the supper bell, but Beth was sleeping now. Not wanting to disturb her, Thomas remained motionless where he was, his hand in hers, waiting for her to wake, restored, and to smile at him again with her pretty eyes.

Points for Discussion

A Certificate for Life-saving

1 Make sure you understand the final question. Why does the boy in the story want to be a hero? Are some people naturally clumsy?

2 Why do you think the author couldn't remember pulling Harry out of the river?

I Likes Screech, I Does

3 The writer keeps repeating: "I knew what I should say. I didn't though." Why doesn't he? In what ways is he different from Spike?

4 "I learned... from this book the English teacher lent me," the writer says. How do you think reading fiction has been useful to *you*? Are there any stories that have proved particularly enlightening to you?

The Coll Doll

5 Then... "The bubble burst". How do you think Julia would have behaved if her mother had not intervened? In what way is this story like *Meeting in Milkmarket* (pp 47-52)? Which did you prefer? Give your reasons.

6 Why does Schol get into a fight? If it is true that he "can tell nobody... Who would understand?", what is the point of this story?

Mort

7 What attracts Mike to Fiona? Explain what Mike means when he says "although I knew I loved Fiona..., I didn't like her very much." What do you think of her?

8 Did you enjoy this story more than *The Coll Doll*?

Meeting in Milkmarket

9 "I did not question whether the thing that we shared could justify its claim to the title of friendship." What does the

word "friendship" mean to you? Do you think your idea of a "friend" changes as you get older? Collect the views of others on this subject.

10 Why was George such a special friend to Stanley? Why does he say that the words 'Georgie like a barefoot girl' "seem to tell the total story of our society"?

The Coming of Maureen Peal

11 Why do the boys taunt Pecola about seeing a man naked? What does Claudia mean, when reminded of seeing her father naked, that she felt "the shame brought on by the absence of shame"?

12 Why do you think Maureen is so friendly towards Pecola after the boys disappear? What causes this relationship to deteriorate?

The Distant One

13 What are the advantages and disadvantages of leaving home and moving a great distance away, instead of staying nearby?

I Spy

14 What will Mrs Stowe tell her son in the morning? Will Charlie tell her he witnessed the events of the night?

15 How do you think Charlie will feel about Mr Stowe in the morning? In what way is son like father?

Where Are You Going, Where Have You Been?

16 Arthur tells Connie, "This is your day set aside for a ride with me and you know it". Is this true? Is there anything Connie could have done to have avoided going with him?

17 Use this dialogue (from page 88) as a starting point to explain why this story is so frightening.

"I ain't made plans for coming in that house where I don't belong but just for you to come out to me, the way you should. Don't you know who I am?"

" 'You're crazy,' she whispered."

Chicken

18 Why is this story so hilarious — or did you find it too nauseating to laugh? Did you spot the dreadful pun?

The Wounded Cormorant

19 Compare this story to the other one written by Liam O'Flaherty (*All Things Come of Age*). They are written from different points of view. How does this affect our reaction in each to the animal in danger?

20 Why did the flock cast out the wounded cormorant? Did the story shock you?

All Things Come of Age

21 You probably wouldn't have expected a story about a baby rabbit to hold your attention. What makes this one successful?

22 Did you notice that we read of the duck's terror before the baby rabbit understands the "nearness of a sinister force"? What is the point of such an arrangement? Why don't we read about the weasel killing the mother?

23 Did you find this a sad story?

Last Rabbit

24 Was it necessary for the old man to get rid of Meg? Why did he kill her in this particular way?

25 Notice that the old man's emotions are hardly described. What does the story tell you about his character?

Meima-Bucha

26 In what ways did the area seem unpleasant? Why was it then "fresh, light and sweet smelling" after the visit?

27 What does the final sentence tell you about Meima-Bucha's family? Why do some children neglect their aged parents? What could they do?

Hurricane Season

28 What do you think this story is mainly about?

Last Love

29 In what ways are Thomas and Beth better off in their old age than Meima-Bucha (pp 116-118) or Meg's owner in *Last Rabbit* (pp 110-114)? Why doesn't it matter to this pair how their children feel about them?

30 Would you call this a sad or happy tale? Explain.

Ideas for Writing

A Certificate for Live-saving

1 Sometimes you can feel better about an occasion on which you made a fool of yourself if you can recount it in a self-mocking, entertaining way. Why doesn't this storyteller do that when he describes his rescue attempt, and his unsuccessful dive? Think of an embarrassing occasion in your own past. Write about it, first describing what happened and how you felt about it, and then by turning it into a joke.

2 There are, however, some amusing lines in this story; for example, the fact that the boy won the breast-stroke championship only because "the three lads in front were disqualified...". Look back through the story and see what other colourful phrases you like. Write them down.

I Likes Screech, I Does

3 Describe Spike Lewis.

4 How does the writer feel about the accident? How do we know this? Can we say whose fault it was?

The Coll Doll

5 "I felt I was walking a foot above the ground." Why does the author feel like this? How many times in life has that happened to you? Describe an occasion which has filled you with great pleasure.

Mort

6 Imagine that Fiona keeps a diary. Write her brief entries for the days that are covered in this story. Try to capture her style of talking.

7 Have you ever let a friend down, or told a lie that you still feel guilty about? See if you can turn the incident into a story.

Meeting in Milkmarket

8 Think back over your own childhood and describe one particular friendship. Or if you have a friend whom you have known for a long time, decide on an experience you shared together some years ago, and compare what you both write about it. There might be a group of you, for instance, who went together on a school outing.

The Coming of Maureen Peal

9 Write down your impressions of Claudia and Frieda. Why is Maureen "not worthy" of the intense hatred the sisters feel?

10 Read the last paragraph again. See if you can answer the questions "What was the secret? What did we lack? Why was it important? And so what?" Can you explain what the "*Thing* to fear" was? Is this still true of today's society?

The Distant One

11 Write the letter which Mrs Austin receives at the end of this story.

12 "Closer than anything...". Was this really true of Albert and Leroy? What makes children in a family close? Describe your relationship with another member of your family as honestly as you can.

I Spy

13 Explain the full implication of the title *I Spy*.

14 See if you can work out how the author has created the atmosphere of tension in this story. Then use the techniques to write a story in which you witness an event which the persons involved thought was secret or clandestine.

Where Are You Going, Where Have You Been?

15 Write a description of Connie and her family. What does the author think of Connie? What do *you* feel about her?

16 Continue the story.

Chicken

17 Why would this story make a succesful radio play? See if you can tape it.

The Wounded Cormorant

18 Look at the first paragraph. There is a simile — a comparison using the word "like" — which is particularly effective. Can you explain why? Find two other similes in the story and state why they are apt. In what other ways is the cruelty of nature already suggested in the opening?

19 Think about other stories of animals which you have read. Try and analyse why you have enjoyed some more than others.

All Things Come of Age

20 The author makes considerable use of the five senses in describing the scene. Which are the most predominant? See if you can describe a natural scene in as much detail.

Last Rabbit

21 Write or tape the conversation that Jenny and Tom would have that evening.

Meima-Bucha

22 Write about how the author felt during the visit to Meima-Bucha. Why did she remember her "feelings with disgust and fear"?

23 Write about what you think could be the best and worst aspects of growing old.

Hurricane Season

24 Why has Jacob become so obsessed with the weather? Do you know an old person with an obsession? Is it different from what a young person might have? Describe the Everetts' home and what it means to each of them.

25 Give the account that Francis might give of his parents, and then one that an unsympathetic onlooker might give.

Last Love

26 Write the letters Beth would have sent to her daughter Annie soon after they moved into the flat and then about a month later. Do the same for the letters Thomas would have sent to his son Allan.

The Authors

Sid Chaplin was born in the mining area of South West Durham, and went to work at the pit when he was 15. Most of his working life was spent as a maintenance man, but in later years he worked in the public relations department of the National Coal Board. His stories and novels have become very popular, and there are two collections: *The Leaping Lad and other stories* (available in *Longman Imprint Books*) and *The Bachelor Uncle and other stories*. *The Watchers and the Watched*, *Sam in the Morning*, and *The Day of the Sardine* are his most famous novels, and a popular stage musical was based on his stories: *Close the Coalhouse Door*. Especially recommended is his collection of articles and descriptive pieces: *The Smell of Sunday Dinner*. Sid Chaplin recounts how he first became a story writer − by having to tell stories to his younger brother and sisters to help them to sleep at night. His work comes out of his observation of life in mining areas, and is a most vivid and moving collection of fiction.

Peter Tinniswood is a British novelist, playwright and television scriptwriter. Formerly he worked as a journalist with the *Sheffield Star*, the *Sheffield Telegraph*, the *Liverpool Daily Post* and the *Western Mail*. He has won awards for two of his novels: *A Touch of Daniel* (Authors' Club First Novel Award 1969) and *I Didn't Know You Cared* (Royal Society of Literature Award 1973).

Walter Macken Born in Galway in 1915, Walter Macken has been called "one of Ireland's greatest novelists". His first writing was for the theatre, and he started writing plays when he was seventeen. His theatrical career took him from Galway to London, and to Dublin. He has written several novels, but his short stories are particularly well known, especially the volumes called *The Coll Doll and Other Stories* and *God Made Sunday*. In this series you can read other stories in *Loves, Hopes, and Fears*, and *Irish Short Stories*. He died in 1968.

John Wain was born at Stoke-on-Trent, in the centre of the area of North Staffordshire known as the Potteries, in March 1925. He was educated at The High School, Newcastle-under-Lyme and at St John's College, Oxford. He was Fereday Fellow at St John's from 1946 to 1949, and from 1949 to 1951 he was Lecturer in English Literature at the University of Reading. But his interest in writing prompted him to resign from full-time lecturing to become a freelance author and critic. Since 1953, when his first novel, *Hurry On Down*, appeared, John Wain has produced a large volume of writing. *The Contenders* (1958), *Strike the Father Dead* (1962), and *A Winter In The Hills* (1970) are novels; *A Wood Carved In a Sill* (1956), *Weep Before God* (1961) and *The Shape of Feng* (1972) are poetry collections; and his critical writing has included *The Living World of Shakespeare* (1964). In 1973 John was elected Professor of Poetry at Oxford University.

John Wickham was born in Barbados, where he was educated. For a while he worked with the World Meteorological Organisation in Geneva. He has also lived in Canada, but considers Barbados his home. He is recognised as a skilful short story writer, and especially one who can realistically dramatise the racial theme.

Toni Morrison was born in Ohio, USA, and studied at Howard and Cornell Universities. She worked as an instructor of English at Texas Southern University and then at Howard, before becoming an editor with a New York book publishers. She received acclaim for her two novels written from the point of view of a black female: *The Bluest Eye* (1971) and *Sula* (1974). Her next novel, *Song of Solomon*, was winner of the National Book Critics Circle Award. All her works evoke "the sights, the sounds, and the rituals of the black past", and capture the resentment, humour and passion of black people living in small-town America.

Michael Anthony was born in a small village in Trinidad. He went to a Roman Catholic school, and left at fifteen to work in a foundry. When he was twenty-two he emigrated to England, eventually becoming a teleprinter operator at the famous news agency, Reuter. He started writing articles, poems and short stories, and his first was published in the West Indian literary magazine, *Bim*, in 1959. Later he returned to Trinidad, working in the publications department of a big oil company. Since then he has moved to work in the Trinidadian Ministry of Culture. He has published many novels, including *The Year in San Fernando* and *Green Days by the River*. His short stories have been collected in *Cricket in the Road*.

Graham Greene was born in Berkhampstead, Hertfordshire, son of the Headmaster of Berkhampstead School. He once stated that a major writer is obsessed. His own obsession stemmed from his experiences at the School, where he felt he encountered people who bore the stamp of absolute evil. Heaven became credible to him because he had lived in hell. He left home after an unhappy adolescence, and found his niche as a staff member of *The Times*. He later moved to *The Spectator* as Film Critic and subsequently Literary Editor. Besides his short stories, he has written plays, fiction for children and many novels. He calls his novels of politics and intrigue "entertainments" — they certainly show his talents as a storyteller. It is difficult to single out titles from Graham Greene's successes, but well recommended are *Brighton Rock*, *The Power and the Glory*, *The Heart of the Matter* and *The Quiet American*.

Joyce Carol Oates is an American novelist, playwright, poet and literary critic. She is Associate Professor of English at the University of Windsor, Ontario. Her volumes of short stories include *The Goddess and Other Women* (1974), *Crossing the Border* (1976) and *Nightside* (1977).

Alan Sillitoe was born in Nottingham in 1928. He went to various elementary schools and at fourteen left school to work at the Raleigh bicycle factory in Coventry. He was called up for National Service at eighteen and joined the RAF, spending nearly two years in Malaya. Then he caught tuberculosis and spent eighteen months in hospital. During this time he began to write, but it was not until 1958 that his first novel, *Saturday Night and Sunday Morning*, was published. Since then he has written a variety of books, including collections of poetry and short stories, as well as novels such as *The General* and *The Death of William Posters*.

Liam O'Flaherty is an Irish writer who is thought by many to be one of the greatest short story writers of the century. He was born in the remote Aran Islands in 1896, and knows the difficult life of the Irish peasant at first hand. After secondary school he went to the University College of Dublin, and soon after the start of the First World War entered the Irish Guards. Two years later he came out of the army shellshocked. He then returned to the Aran Islands for a while, but started travelling. He has written fourteen novels and a huge collection of short stories. His best known novels are *The Informer*, *Skerrett*, and *Famine*. Readers are especially recommended to try his collections of short stories.

James Cunningham was born in Glasgow in 1928. He was educated at Glasgow High School and graduated from Glasgow University with an MA in history and economics in 1952. After short spells as a teacher and as a purser aboard steamers on the River Clyde, James Cunningham began a career as an insurance salesman. After this false start, he joined the *Glasgow Herald* as a sub-editor. He became gossip columnist on this newspaper, before moving to his current post as features editor on the *Daily Record*. 'Last Rabbit' was published for the first time in *The Guardian* on 7 July 1979. Some of his short stories have appeared in the *Glasgow Herald*; others have been read on BBC Radio.

Ruth Fainlight Born in New York, Ruth Fainlight was educated at various schools in England and America. Her main training was in Art Colleges in Birmingham and Brighton. She married the writer Alan Sillitoe, and they have one son and an adopted daughter. She had a volume of poetry published in 1966 called *Cages*, and other volumes followed. As well as poems and novels, she has translated with her husband Lope de Vega's famous Spanish play *Fuenteovejuna*. This story comes from her collection *Daylife and Nightlife* (published by André Deutsch).

Edgar Mittelholzer His first writing was at the age of twenty-nine. He was living and working in the small coastal town of New Amsterdam in Guyana "doing odd jobs for the customs; checking drums of petrol off-loaded from schooners, and even acting as cinema inspector at a frowzy local cinema". After the publication of his first novel *Corentyne Thunder* (published in the Caribbean Writers Series by Heinemann Educational Books in

1941, three years after it had been written), he moved to Trinidad, where he lived until 1948. *Corentyne Thunder* was the first novel to explore Guyanese peasant life, and Mittelholzer drew on his own upbringing in Guyana for this book. His novels are very famous; after the first, *Morning at the Office* (1951), came *The Children of Kayawana* (1952), and *The Life and Death of Sylvia* (1953). Mittelholzer was of mixed parentage, and felt himself caught between two cultures. His tensions were great, and he committed suicide in 1958.

Angela Huth has written several novels: *South of the Lights, Sun Child, Virginia Fly is Drowning, Nowhere Girl,* as well as several plays for radio and television. Living in Wiltshire, she is a regular broadcaster and television performer.

To the Teacher

Most teachers of English agree that the short story is not only one of the great literary forms of the late twentieth century, but also that it is a form particularly suited for classroom study: writing of high literary merit, often by important authors and frequently exploring serious and adult themes, can be read, responded to, and appreciated by a wide range of pupils. Many collections in this series have been built around short stories, but one was especially planned for readers in the older classes in secondary schools for whom much literature seems remote and difficult. That book was *Loves, Hopes, and Fears*, published in 1975, and very widely read.

This collection has been planned as complementary to it. The seventeen stories have been chosen firstly for their literary merit, and secondly because they are direct and accessible. Almost all the authors are famous exponents of their craft, many of them major literary figures. Particular care has been taken to include stories that will help break the anglo-centricism of many literature collections, thus the black experience in the USA, the West Indies, and this country is one of the underlying themes. Similarly, a number of stories by women authors have been included.

Linking the stories are interconnections of theme: the experiences of growing up, love, old age, the barriers of class, people, and animals. In most of the stories the authors have focussed on a meeting or a parting, to look into the human spirit. I hope that many school readers will not only enjoy these stories as literature, but sense in them the authors' response to people.

Although the stories have been chosen for their comparative directness and ease of language, they have also been chosen to be challenging and to be well worth close study.

M.M.

A Choice of Books

In reading, one title leads on to another, and we often find most pleasure in picking up a book which in some way or other has been prompted by what we have just read and enjoyed. Listed here is a small choice of books which in various ways touch on similar experiences and ideas to those of the stories in this collection. It would be especially good for members of a group working with this collection each to read a different book from this list and to compare notes later.

AJEBO, KEITH, *Black, Lives, White World*, Cambridge University Press

ANTHONY, MICHAEL, *A Year in San Fernando*, Heinemann Caribbean Writers Series

ANTHONY, MICHAEL, *Cricket on the Road*, Heinemann Caribbean Writers Series

ANTHONY, MICHAEL, *Green Days by the River*, Heinemann Caribbean Writers Series

BANKS, LYNN REID, *The L-Shaped Room*, Longman *(Imprint Books)*

BARSTOW, STAN, *A Kind of Loving*, Hutchinson

BARSTOW, STAN, *Joby*, Bodley Head

BARSTOW, STAN, *Watchers on the Shore*, Bodley Head

BARSTOW, STAN, *The Human Element*, Longman *(Imprint Books)*

BATES, H.E., *The Good Corn and other stories*, Longman *(Imprint Books)*

BUCKTON, CHRIS, editor, *The Experience of Parenthood*, Longman *(Imprint Books)*

CALLOW, PHILIP, *Going to the Moon*, MacGibbon & Kee

CALLOW, PHILIP, *Native Ground*, Heinemann

DAVIES, MARILYN, and MARLAND, MICHAEL, editors, *Breaking Away*, Longman *(Imprint Books)*

GREENE, GRAHAM, *Stories*, Bodley Head

GREENE, GRAHAM, *Brighton Rock*, Heinemann Educational

HANLEY, CLIFFORD, *A Taste of Too Much*, Blackie

HEMINGWAY, ERNEST, *A Hemingway Selection*, Longman
(Imprint Books)

HILL, SUSAN, *A Bit of Singing and Dancing*, Hamish Hamilton

KAMM, JOSEPHINE, *Young Mother*, Heinemann

LESSING, DORIS, *The Grass is Singing*, Heinemann
Educational

LESSING, DORIS, *Nine African Stories*, Longman *(Imprint
Books)*

MACKEN, WALTER, *God Made Sunday and other stories*,
Macmillan

MARLAND, EILEEN and MICHAEL, editors, *Friends and
Families*, Longman *(Imprint Books)*

MARLAND, MICHAEL, editor, *Caribbean Stories*, Longman
(Imprint Books)

MARLAND, MICHAEL, editor, *The Experience of Love*,
Longman *(Imprint Books)*

MARLAND, MICHAEL, editor, *Loves, Hopes, and Fears*,
Longman *(Imprint Books)*

MARLAND, MICHAEL, editor, *The Experience of Colour*,
Longman *(Imprint Books)*

NAIPAUL, V.S., *Miguel Street*, Heinemann Caribbean Writers

NAIPAUL, V.S., *A Flag on the Island*, André Deutsch/Penguin

NAUGHTON, BILL, *Late Night in Watling Street*, Longman
(Imprint Books)

NAUGHTON, BILL, *One Small Boy*, Longman *(Imprint Books)*

SELVON, SAMUEL, *The Lonely Londoners*, Longman
Caribbean

SELVON, SAMUEL, *Ways of Sunlight*, Longman Caribbean

SILLITOE, ALAN, *A Sillitoe Selection*, Longman *(Imprint Books)*

SILLITOE, ALAN, *The Loneliness of the Long-Distance Runner*,
Longman *(Heritage of Literature)*

WAIN, JOHN, *A John Wain Selection*, Longman *(Imprint Books)*

WATERHOUSE, KEITH, *There is a Happy Land*, Longman
(Imprint Books)

WRIGHT, RICHARD, *Black Boy*, Longman *(Imprint Books)*

Longman Imprint Books
General Editor: Michael Marland CBE

Titles in the series

I'm the King of the Castle   Susan Hill
Sliding   Leslie Norris
Juliet Bravo   *edited by* Alison Leake
Still Waters and other plays   Julia Jones
Television Comedy Scripts   *edited by* Roy Blatchford
Meetings and Partings   *edited by* Alison Leake
A Laurie Lee Selection   *edited by* Chris Buckton

*   Cassette available

Acknowledgements

We are grateful to the following for permission to reproduce copyright material:

Jonathan Cape Ltd & the author, Liam O'Flaherty for the short story 'The Wounded Cormorant' from *The Short Stories of Liam O'Flaherty;* the author's agents for the short story 'A Certificate for Lifesaving' by Sid Chaplin from *The Bachelor Uncle & Other Stories* pub. Carcanet Press; Collins Publishers for the short story 'Last Love' by Angela Huth from *Monday Lunch & Other Stories;* the author, James Cunningham for his short story 'Last Rabbit'; André Deutsch Ltd for the short story 'Meima Bucha' by Ruth Fainlight from *Daylight & Nightlife* 1971; the author's agents for the short story 'I Spy' by Graham Greene from *Collected Stories* pub. The Bodley Head & Wm. Heinemann; Michael Joseph Ltd for the short story 'I Likes Screech, I Does' by Peter Tinniswood from *Dandelion Clocks* ed. Bradley & Jamieson; Macmillan Accounts & Administration Ltd for the short story 'The Coll Doll' by Walter Macken from *The Coll Doll & Other Stories;* the author's agents for an extract from *Hurricane Season* by Edgar Mittelholzer, © Mrs Jacqueline Ives; the author's agents for the short 'Where are you Going, Where have you Been' by Joyce Carol Oates, © 1966 by Joyce Carol Oates; the author, Liam O'Flaherty & Wolfhound Press for the short story 'All Things Come of Age' from *Short Stories − The Pedlar's Revenge* 1976, 1981 Wolfhound Press; the author's agents for the short story 'Chicken' by Alan Sillitoe from *Guzman, Go Home* pub. W.H. Allen, © 1968 by Alan Sillitoe; the author's agents for the short story 'Mort' by John Wain from *You Can't Keep out the Darkness* © John Wain, by kind permission of Curtis Brown Ltd; the author, John Wickham for his short story 'Meeting in Milkmarket'.

Though every effort has been made, we are unable to trace the copyright holders of *The Distant One* by Michael Anthony & *The Coming of Maureen Peal* by Toni Morrison, and would appreciate any information which would enable us to do so.